Greg Strauss – South Afric competitive bodybuilder, personal trainer, gym owner, equipment designer and author brings you 26 years of experience in the form of the Eleven Minute Workout.

"In a field plagued with fads and misinformation, the EMW provides a fresh new approach to attaining total fitness."

The best **$1-a-minute** you can spend to improve your health.

Achieve maximum results with the absolute minimum time and effort needed.

The best of the best exercises everyone should do!
<u>The exercises your body cannot do without.</u>

"Great for Traveling"

No equipment required the EMW utilizes fundamental body movements to show you in a clear and concise manner how to achieve total fitness in only eleven minutes a day.

"Our whole family does the program"

Greg will show you the exercises that will produce the greatest benefits of fitness, function and health with the least amount of time and effort.

"Fits into a busy schedule perfectly"

VRI index shows how you get the benefits of 1 hour of exercise in only 11 minutes. This high intensity program helps to increase your metabolism, lose weight and burn fat.

According to the American College of Sports Medicine, "Every U.S. adult should accumulate 30 minutes or more of moderate-intensity physical activity on most, preferably all, days of the week." — The 11 minute workout is a great way to begin.

The
Eleven Minute Workout

Also referred to as the
EMW

© 2003 by Gregory E. Strauss and Motion Fitness

All illustrations, images and photographs are the © by Gregory E. Strauss and Motion Fitness

Published in the United States of America
Motion Fitness
119 E. Palatine Road, Suite 205
Palatine, IL 60067
Toll-Free: 1-877-668-4664
Email: sales@motionfitness.com
Visit us on the Web at www.motionfitness.com

Library of Congress Control Number: 2003111483

Strauss, Gregory E
    Eleven Minute Workout

All rights reserved under International Copyright Conventions. No part of this manuscript or associated work contained therein may be reproduced or transmitted, in any form or by any means, electronically or mechanically, including photocopying, recording, or by any information storage and retrieval system, without specific permission in writing from the publisher.

ISBN 0-9744568-0-2

Printed in the United States of America
10 9 8 7 6 5 4 3 2 1

Warning & Disclaimer

Consult with your doctor before
attempting these exercises.

The information in this book reflects the author's experience and current research, and is not intended to replace individual medical or professional advice. Before beginning this or any exercise or nutritional program, consult with your physician or other appropriate health professional. This program contains exercises that, depending upon your physical condition, may be hazardous to your health. User assumes all risk for performing the exercises described in this book. No guarantee's are expressed or implied. Use of this book constitutes a covenant not to bring any lawsuit or action for injury caused by performing exercises illustrated in this course. If you do not wish to be bound by the above, you may return this book to the dealer.

I wrote this book for everybody

You are about to embark on a journey of immense proportions. You are now opening the gate and stepping into the path.

The longer you stay on the path the better it gets. You need to start out slowly at first. You cannot rush the journey. Only day by day can you apply yourself and enjoy the experience.

Results will come quickly with proper and safe application of the principles contained in this book.

Contents

Introduction	13
What is the Eleven Minute Workout	14
How the Eleven Minute Workout was developed	16
Why you should do the Eleven Minute Workout	17
Is Eleven minutes enough?	18
Why only 30 seconds per exercise segment	24
Intensity – The key to getting results	26
Does it mathematically compute?	29
Which exercises and why?	31
Breakdown of the elements	37
Beginner Workout instructions	39
An important reminder	65
Intermediate Workout instructions	66
Advanced Workout instructions	85
Recipe for success	104
The Mind/Body connection in fitness	105
Tracking Your Progress	105
Progress Potential	107
Stress and Exercise	110
Diet and Exercise	112
Additional Tips	114
References	116
Glossary	118
Online Support	120

About the Author

Greg Strauss was born in Johannesburg, South Africa in 1961. At 16, while attending King Edward VII Boys High School he became enamored with bodybuilding and physical fitness.

In 1979 he was drafted into the South African Air Force where he completed the Drill Instructor Training Program. The additional education in Anatomy, Kinesiology and Exercise Physiology further added to strengthen his resolve about physical fitness. He continued pursuing his bodybuilding agenda and after completing his time in the Air Force, sought to further his career in amateur bodybuilding competitions. Success came in 1984 and 1985 when he captured a number of bodybuilding titles.

These achievements gave him the thrust to relocate to Los Angeles, California. Greg Strauss pursued the fitness arena. He entered numerous bodybuilding contests and won many awards for his efforts. In the gym his naturally helpful attitude was rewarded with solicitations for instruction on how to exercise. Personal Training became a full time occupation. He started working on his own training formula from which the Eleven Minute Workout was born.

In 1992 he opened the Strauss Fitness Center. Word spread quickly about the service, quality training and value for money he offered. The Strauss Fitness Center provided it's clients with the most accurate and current information possible. Its goal was for clients to experience results from their training in the quickest way possible. Greg was always on the lookout for ways and methods to improve. During this time the refinement of the Eleven Minute Workout was developed - Sophisticated enough to satisfy the professional person, yet clear and concise enough to be accessible to clients of any level.

In September of 1995, Greg Strauss sold his fitness center to focus on developing exercise products and sharing his knowledge of the Health Industry.

Acknowledgment

This book is a project that has spanned 18 years. There are many people to thank for there various contributions. Most importantly are the many personal training clients I have had and whose workouts served as a test-bed for this program. In no particular order I would also like to thank the following people

Dr. Bruce Bell, Leon Chaussee, Kevin Duhe, Richard Graham, Alan Katz and Jerry Simons, Ed Kasanders and Motion Fitness, John Lupo, Arnold Schwarzenegger, Randy and Ryan Sheinbein, Dr Michael Sheps and the Allcare Back Clinic, Steve Smith, and my father Richard Strauss.

Introduction

The purpose of this book is to help you achieve and maintain total fitness in the quickest and most effective way possible.

More than just getting a workout, the EMW will enhance your overall fundamental functional capacity. Functional capacity is the physical health of the body i.e.: when your joints bend the way they are supposed to and your muscles work the way they are supposed to. The combination of these two systems is called the musculo-skeletal system. The bones and the muscles are completely dependant upon one another and when they work at optimum capacity your overall health is enhanced. This is what the EMW aims to do for you. By utilizing exercises that are essentially basic body movements and using when possible more than one bone joint at a time, the bodies athletic ability is improved while giving you a complete workout. Since I tested this program for more than twelve years, I am quite sure that this goal will be accomplished for you.

What is the EMW?

The EMW is a one-hour workout condensed into eleven minutes. After twenty-six years in the health and fitness industry, I have noticed that the average person spends about ten to fifteen minutes per hour doing exercises. The remaining time is spent resting, talking or at the water fountain.

The main elements of the EMW are three of the oldest forms of exercise known to mankind. They are:

Yoga
This tried, tested and time proven form of exercise is unmatched for, amongst other things, it's ability to maintain the flexibility of the body.

Calisthenics
With it's origins in ancient Rome and Greece, this medium has lasted through the ages and still forms the basis of most modern exercise systems.

Boxing
Unappreciated for the longest time, it has only been recently acknowledged for it's ability to produce physical fitness and get results quickly.

To this I have added the most effective elements I have worked with over the past twenty-six years. They are: Circuit Training, Cross Training, Plyometrics, Dynamic Resistance Training, Decompression Mobilization Therapy, Synergy and NLP (Neuro Linguistic Programming).

This information has been consolidated in the twelve most important exercises the human body needs. The physical habits of modern man have played a major role in this choice process.

There are three difficulty levels of the EMW. These levels encapsulate the fitness status of the population at large. They are:

Beginner
People who are just starting a workout program.

Intermediate
People who exercise, play sports or are physically active.

Advanced
The 'hardcore' workout types or sport buffs.

In a field plagued with fads and misinformation, the EMW provides a fresh new approach to attaining total fitness. It clearly addresses all the requirements necessary for total fitness in a unique and interesting way. The EMW also introduces new elements never before adapted to any exercise program. These will be addressed in their own chapters.

How the EMW was developed

This workout was developed over a twelve year period using hundreds of potential exercises and people from all walks of life at my personal training facility. The age range of these people was from eight to eighty.

The goal was to create a workout that would:
1) Achieve maximum results with the absolute minimum time and effort needed.
2) Use only the best piece of equipment – the human body.
3) Achieve total fitness.
4) Enhance your health and the body's functional capacity.
5) Would have to effectively deal with the major physical problems of today's society.
6) Would be able to be done by almost anyone.
7) Would be innovative, creative and fun.
8) Would promote family and group participation.

This was achieved by:
1) Assessing the requirements of physical fitness.
2) Considering the major physical problem's of today's society and their causes.
3) Establishing the most simple, effective exercises to deal with them.
4) Combining the exercises in an innovative and creative way.
5) In the shortest amount of time possible
6) And still attain total fitness.
7) Using only the best piece of equipment – the human body.
8) For family and friends to benefit from and enjoy.

Why you should do the EMW

There are numerous reasons. The most important one being that there is a absolute, definite and distinct connection between your level of fitness and your state of health. Some years ago the Surgeon General made a statement with words to the same effect.

The full benefits of adopting exercise as part of your daily routine can only be realized in the long run. Let me assure you that the results are far more than just having a good looking body. That's just the icing on the cake. The ability to cope with the stress and strain of modern day living is much easier when you have a physically fit and healthy body. In order to attain this, a comprehensive training program such as the EMW is needed.

Remember that you only get one go-around in this lifetime. There are no timeouts, substitutions or action replays and the clock is always ticking. It makes sense then to get as many years as you possibly can and more importantly, healthy years. Watching your children grow and seeing your grandchildren is quality time that has no equal. You owe it to yourself and them to be around for that experience. Take care of your health by exercising daily.

Is eleven minutes enough?

Absolutely! I recommend that your exertion level be about 80-90 % of your maximum ability when doing the EMW. This will ensure that the necessary benefits of total fitness are attained. When it comes to exercise, it's not necessarily how long you workout but what you do that counts. To this end the EMW encompasses total fitness in the simplest and most effective way possible.

The following pages corroborate this theory.

Citation: American Medical News, August 16, 1993
 V36 n31 p5(1)
Title: Recommendations on exercise are modified
Author: Culhane, Charles

Subjects: Exercise Health Aspects
 Heart Disease Prevention
 United States Centers for Disease Control and Prevention Surveys

American College of Sports Medicine reports

Reference # A14450155

Abstract: The American College of Sports Medicine recommends that people should engage in moderate exercise, totaling 30 minutes a day, as a prevention of chronic disease and early death. This is a revision of earlier recommendations of 20 minutes of vigorous daily exercise. However, only 22% of Americans attain even this moderate exercise level, according to a 1990 survey conducted by the Centers of Disease Control and Prevention (CDC).

Is eleven minutes enough? ○ 19

The American Heart Association says that physical inactivity is as great a risk to heart disease as is smoking or high cholesterol! Other statistics of the CDC are provided.

==
Full Text COPYRIGHT American Medical Association, 1993

New advise for patients: You don't have to engage in vigorous exercise for sustained periods to gain substantial health benefits.

The American College of Sports Medicine is prescribing moderate exercise for shorter periods that add up to 30 minutes or more, at least five days a week. Only 22% of Americans now achieve even this moderate level of physical activity, according to the Centers for Disease Control and Prevention. Previous guidelines have emphasized vigorous, continued exercise for at least 20 minutes or more, three to five times a week. That advice was based on studies weighing the impact of such training on physical fitness.

The new recommendations stem primarily from epidemiological studies showing that even moderate physical activity is associated with reduced risks of chronic disease, morbidity and mortality. "We made a mistake, those of us in the exercise science community, by insisting early on that it must be sustained, aerobic activity," said Steven N. Blair, PED, director of epidemiology at the Cooper Institute of Aerobic Research in Dallas. "The most important factor is the total amount of activity that you get, the total calories spent."

Citation: Tufts University Diet and Nutrition Letter, Oct. 1993 v11 v8 p1 (1)

Title: Just do it, even if it's just a little (exercise)

Subject: Exercise Health Aspects

Reference # A13297343

Full Text COPYRIGHT Tufts University Diet and Nutrition Letter 1993

People tend to view it as an all or nothing proposition. They believe that either you get out there and work up a heavy sweat by jogging, swimming or biking for at least 30 minutes straight or you keep yourself parked in front of the TV since anything less than a vigorous workout won't do your body any good. That king of thinking is misguided.

You stand to gain simply by accumulating 30 minutes of moderate to intense physical activity over the course of a day. Using the stairs instead of the elevator, gardening, raking the leaves and walking part of the way to work, are examples. That's the latest from a panel of experts brought together by the Centers for Disease Control and Prevention, as well as the American College of Sports Medicine. They point to a growing body of research suggesting that for a person leading a sedentary lifestyle, just adding 10 minutes of activity here and 5 minutes there reduces the risk of heart disease, high blood pressure, osteoporosis, and breast and colon cancer. Little bits of activity spread throughout the day also help alleviate depression, anxiety and stress.

For people who are extremely sedentary, a little extra activity can reduce the risk of disease as much as quitting smoking, according to Dr. Steven Blair, former president of the American College of Sports Medicine and one of the experts who served on the panel.

Currently, only an estimated one out of five Americans engages in half an hour's worth of daily exercise.

Of course, the new advice does not mean that avid exercisers who make a habit of walking, jogging, swimming or biking for at least 20 to 30 minutes several times a week should cut back. It's no secret to habitual exercisers that working out not only keeps you healthy over the long run but also keeps you looking and feeling good. Still, for those who are not interested in becoming athletes but simply want to stave off chronic diseases, a little activity here and there appears to do the trick.

Incidentally, physically active people tend to outlive inactive people, even if they start their activity late in life.

Citation: Health Facts, Sept. 1993 v18 n172 pl (2)

Title: Vigorous exercise not necessary (to gain substantial
   health benefits).

Subject: Exercise Physiological Aspects

Reference #: A13295563

Full Text COPYRIGHT Center for Medical Consumers Inc. 1993

A newly revised exercise recommendation may encourage more people to get off the couch. Substantial health benefits can be gained by regular moderate exercise, according to the American College of Sports Medicine. The ACSM's earlier guidelines, which had advised continued vigorous exercise lasting 20 minutes or more three to five times a week, were based on studies that zeroed in on physical fitness.

Now research has found that exercising moderately can greatly reduce the risks of numerous chronic diseases and their related disabilities. The new ACSM recommendations are: engage in moderate exercise like swimming, running, walking, dancing, tennis, cycling and any physical activity that adds up to 30 minutes or more at least five days a week. "A person could meet this entire standard by walking two miles a day briskly," said Russell Pate, Ph.D., and ACSM President.

Moderate exercise also appears to be sufficient for women concerned about preserving bone strength, according to a preliminary study in Medicine and Science in Sports and Exercise (Vol. 24, No 11, pp 1190-1194).

All the participants in the study, conducted at the University of Missouri at Columbia, were sedentary women just past menopause, a time when bone loss begins to accelerate. They were divided into three groups: one remained sedentary, the second engaged in regular high impact activities, such as jogging, jumping jacks and/or aerobic dancing: and the third did low impact exercise, such as walking or modified jumping jacks.

At the one-year follow-up, the sedentary women showed a significant decrease in bone density, a finding that would be expected amongst inactive women. An unexpected finding, however, was the lack of difference between low and high impact exercises. Although high impact activity is widely thought to be necessary to stress the bones enough to prevent bone thinning, low impact exercise was found to be just as effective in maintaining bone density. Both exercise groups worked out for 20 minutes, three times a week. Low impact exercise carries the added benefit of an injury rate that is lower than that of high impact activity.

Why only 30 seconds per exercise segment?

With the exception of the Salutation, which takes one minute, all the exercises are done for only 30 seconds at a time. After many attempts to find the right combination and time frame of each exercise, it appeared that 30 seconds was sufficient to fatigue the working muscles when controlled speed was introduced. Controlled speed of the exercise being performed produces an isotonic effect and is necessary for safety and maximum repetitions to produce Intensity, which in turn produces results. Thirty seconds also works best regardless of exercise level (beginner, intermediate, advanced) and age, sex and weight.

It is reasonable to expect, in time, to do approximately 30 repetitions of each exercise. From another angle this can be viewed as 3 sets of 10 repetitions which is quite normal in an exercise program. If the EMW were broken up into these segments, with rest periods added, it would take about an hour to complete. This gets back to my earlier statement about **the EMW being a one-hour workout in 11 minutes.**

So why then do three sets as one set in thirty seconds? The answer is quite simple. It produces a much greater VRI (Volume of Repetition Intensity). With each repetition the intensity increases exponentially. With the second method, peak intensity is not reached, therefore less VRI. The chart on the following page demonstrates the difference between the two.

Note: 30 repetitions is used as an example. You may, depending on your fitness level, be able to do more or less than 30 repetitions in any exercise.

Don't push it, do what is comfortable and natural!

Why only 30 seconds per exercise segment ○ 25

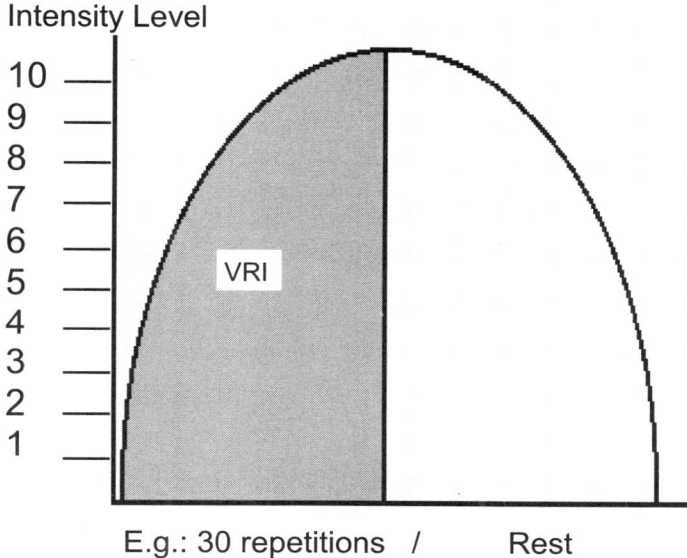

E.g.: 30 repetitions / Rest

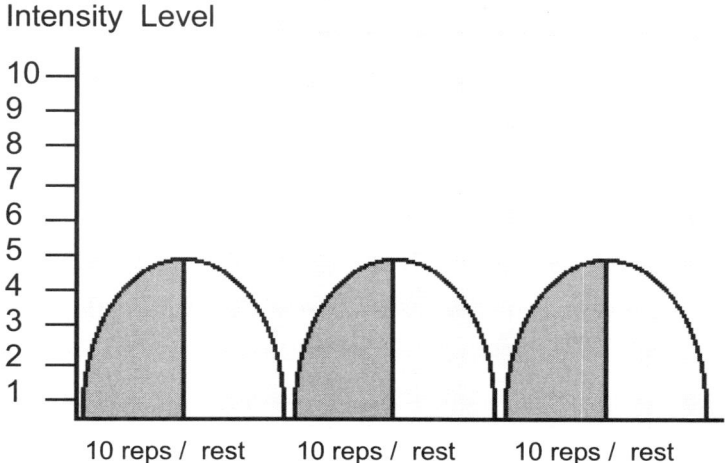

10 reps / rest   10 reps / rest   10 reps / rest

The shaded areas show the VRI as it accumulates during the exercise performance. It's clear to see that the first method is much more effective in producing the VRI necessary to get results.

Intensity - The key to getting results -

Intensity is defined as "...the magnitude of force or energy per unit area..." As it relates to exercise: it is how hard the muscles work at any given point in time. That point is constantly increasing with each additional repetition of the various exercises. This produces the Intensity required to get results. The higher the Intensity level, the shorter the workout needed to attain results. The chart below shows the total VRI of the EMW.

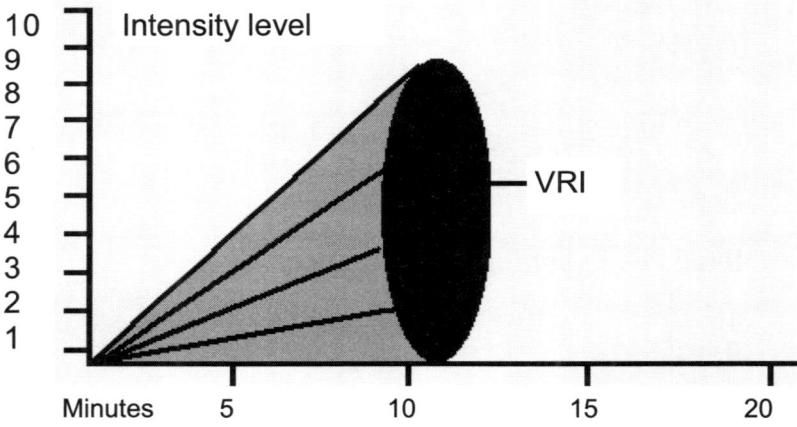

The Intensity level is determined by the recommendation that you perform the EMW at 80-90% of your physical and mental ability.

Common exercise devices that promote 'easy' exercise, normally in one simple (sic) movement, have very low intensity factors. The body will adjust to this within a few weeks and it's also very boring. In order to continue getting results one has to drastically increase the amount of time that you spend on the device and it becomes time prohibitive. We then lose interest and tend to put it off.

The EMW on the other hand has a variety of exercises to constantly keep you stimulated. Let's face it, variety is the spice of life. As you progress and complete more and more repetitions the VRI increases and this is what produces results.

The graph below shows the Intensity levels of the EMW exercises. Turn the page sideways and notice how it flows in peaks and valleys which are instrumental in challenging the body to produce results.

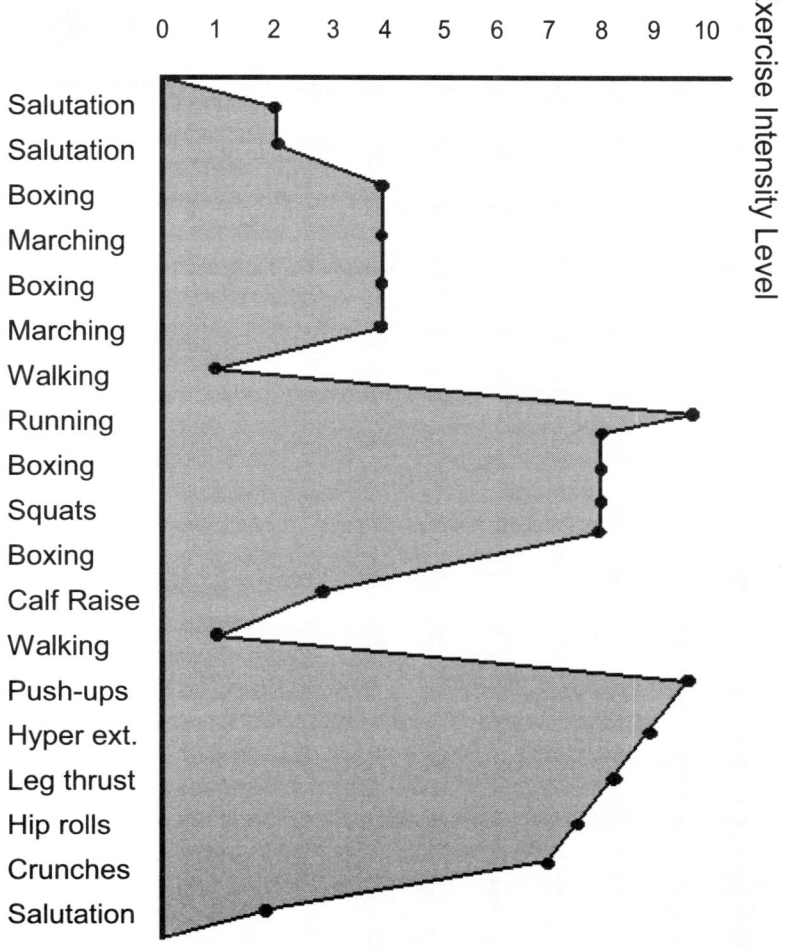

Remember this: performing only one movement or exercise cannot attain total fitness. The body needs to be stimulated in different ways to attain the five key factors of total fitness which are: Flexibility, Speed, Strength, Coordination and Endurance. The muscles need to be trained in these different aspects in order to effectively function in each aspect of total fitness. Only one movement or exercise cannot accomplish this no matter how hard you try or how much time you spend doing it.

The EMW effectively addresses all five aspects of total fitness in a comprehensive selection of exercises uniquely combined in a systematic time frame that is conducive to modern times. In this way the EMW unequivocally supersedes the common exercise devices of our time!

The EMW
Does it mathematically compute?

Some years ago I started working on an equation that would justify the EMW. Essentially what I was trying to do was define the 'work' in 'workout'. So I began with w = f x d, i.e.: work = force x distance. How would this apply to the EMW and how would it justify Intensity? Here is what I came up with.

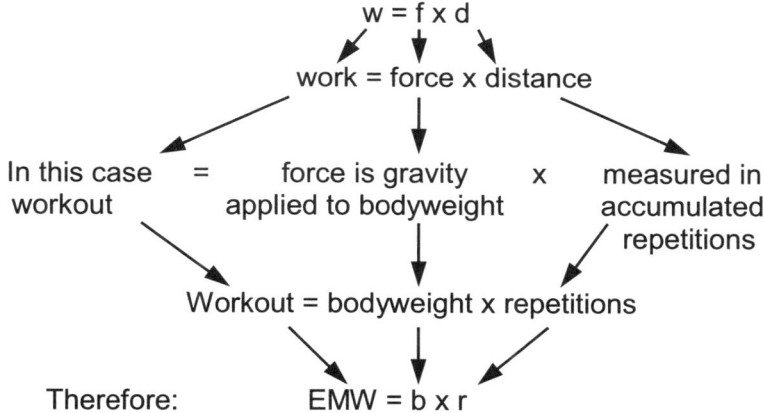

The result is that the benefits of the EMW are derived by your bodyweight multiplied by the number of repetitions you complete. This combination ultimately produces Intensity, the key to getting results!

Reduced to it's most basic elements, the equation shows the intricate blend of factors that is the nucleus of the EMW.

As I see it, there are two primary ways to exercise. The first and most commonly used is the *low intensity/ long duration* type workout. The premise behind this concept is to burn calories and hopefully fat during the workout. This places the focus primarily on the endurance aspect of total fitness.

On the other hand, the concept of *high intensity/ short duration* type workout is less known. It seems a difficult concept to grasp as the 'more is better' syndrome prevails in our society. When it comes to exercising for health benefits, we have seen that more is not necessarily better.

The theory of high *intensity/short duration* can be explained like this. According to Dr. Kenneth Cooper of the Cooper Institute of Aerobics Research in Dallas, Texas, an aerobic workout at 100% maximum effort takes 4 minutes to complete. At 60-70% of maximum capacity it takes 20 minutes. Now there are 11 minutes of sustained movement in the EMW that induces an aerobic/anaerobic effect on the body, meaning that it relies heavily on muscle involvement and requires large amounts of oxygen. Being that the suggested level of Intensity is 80-90 percent of maximum capacity, it is reasonable to assume that it meets Dr. Cooper's requirements for aerobic involvement. Thus addressing the endurance aspect of the EMW.

Flexibility has always been measured by you being able to touch your toes. This is addressed in the Salutation.

Strength has always been measured by how many push-ups you can do. Hence push-ups in the EMW.

Speed has always been measured by how fast you can run. Hence running (on the spot) in the EMW.

Coordination is required by all of the above. It is developed by continuous effort.

Through many years of research and development I can say with confidence that all the aspects of total fitness are completely addressed in the EMW.

Which exercises and why?

There are only twelve exercises in the EMW. Each has been carefully selected through a process of elimination for it's contribution to the 5 elements that make up total fitness (flexibility, strength, speed, coordination, endurance). All this adds up to functional capacity and ultimately health improvement. To all of this I have added the 'Mind/Body Connection' which, as far as I know, has never before been added to an exercise program. This topic will be addressed in it's own chapter. Page 105.

Over the past twenty-six years I have watched people exercising. All exercise will benefit you somehow, although I am quite sure that the benefits of some are greater than others. Here then, in my humble opinion are the best of the best. The exercises your body cannot do without. The exercises that will produce the greatest benefits of fitness, function and health with the least amount of time and effort.

The physical habits of modern society and the dynamics of the world in which we live have influenced this choice process. Without question, the most detrimental of these habits is the fact that we spend way too much time in the seated position. In this position, the lower back is compromised, the stomach muscles sag, the hips and buttocks expand, the thigh muscles atrophy, the metabolism slows down and the neck and shoulders become overburdened with the tasks of the arms and hands. In the meantime stress is accumulating in the body.

The EMW is designed to offset all these degrading effects and re-establish harmony to your constitution.

All of the exercises have been modified so as to meet the needs and the overall goal of the EMW. Many exercises were tried and tested during the twelve years of research and development. These twelve exercises were chosen for their outstanding contribution to the goals of the EMW.

1) Push-ups

My experience has shown that this is the exercise that most people avoid. It has also been showed to me that people generally dislike the exercise they need the most. No single exercise is more needed than the push-up. Every muscle in the body plays a role in push-ups to some degree. Granted the pushing muscles are doing most of the work and thank goodness for that. Flabby underarms, sagging chests and breasts, a protruding abdomen, a weak neck and all the other muscles will function in synergy. That is, they will develop in a way that is in absolute harmony with the design of the human body.

2) The Sun Salutation

I refer to it in the program as the Salutation. This is the contribution of Yoga to the EMW and it makes up three minutes of the workout. It takes one minute to perform and is done twice to start the workout and once to finish. This coincides with the philosophy of stretching before and after exercise. Every basic functional movement of the body is explored. All the muscles are fully stretched and the joints are lubricated. Breathing deeply will calm your constitution. Crucial elements of Decompression Mobilization Therapy are in the Salutation, which is a progressive system of very unique exercises, which promote mobility, flexibility and strength of the spine.

3) Squats

In an issue of Muscle and Fitness magazine, Arnold Schwarzenegger referred to squats as the most essential component of any leg training program. This is also one of the Decompression Mobilization Therapy exercises and also one of the three movements that constitute the sport of Powerlifting. This absolutely fantastic basic human function will condition every muscle in your legs, buttocks, hips and lower back. It will also increase the capacity of both your heart and lungs. Finally the lower back area in the region of your tailbone, known as the Sacroiliac (the body's personal shock absorber) will be stretched, strengthened and full mobility of the hips and knees will be promoted. In societies where the squat is performed as a sitting or resting position, very seldom is the osteo-arthritic knee ever seen.

Throughout history men and women have been measured by the strength of their backs. Having a strong back is the key element to having a strong body. The muscles that surround the spine and their strength are imperative to holding the discs and vertebrae together. These disks and vertebrae tend to move out of place when the muscles surrounding them become weak or imbalanced in strength. Although strong abdominals are important to back stability, they are less important than strong legs are to back strength. This is easily explained by looking at the worlds strongest men such as Olympic Weight lifters and professional Powerlifters. To reach this level of athletic prowess requires an exceptionally strong back. These strength dynamos are also known for having protruding abdomens since they don't train this body part as part of their conditioning routine. Their leg and back strength is a direct result of these athletes having performed thousands upon thousands of squats such as are done in the EMW.

4) Hyper-extensions
This exercise will directly strengthen the pulling muscles of the upper body, especially the lower back, the Rhomboids (posture muscles located between the shoulder blades), posterior deltoids, the buttocks, hips and the hamstrings (rear part of the thigh). The back muscles that surround and stabilize the spine will gain the most benefit from this movement.

5) Boxing
Unappreciated and underestimated is the only way to describe the skill and conditioning that will come from boxing. Every muscle of your upper body, including the hips and waistline, will be challenged and taxed by throwing punches in rapid succession. For productive purposes, I have selected the 'jab' since it uses the most muscles and the highest amount of punches can be thrown per thirty second round, which in turn produces the Intensity required. Finally, you are exhausting the upper body muscles aerobically before anaerobic fatigue takes place in the latter segment of the workout.

6) Running
The ability of the human body to perform in so many different areas of physical function is design perfection personified. Running is absolutely necessary for total leg strength, abdominal and hip conditioning and a super cardio pulmonary pump. This too, will aerobically fatigue the leg muscles before anaerobic exhaustion during squats and calf raises. Research has shown that this factor contributes to maximum intensity.

7) HFL Leg Thrusts
Without question this is one of the most innovative and effective lower abdominal conditioning exercise to come out in recent years. This is very important because of the synergistical sequence the abs need to be trained

in; lower abs, the sides and then the upper abs.* This exercise is especially challenging and will take a few tries to get it right. Be persistent and you will develop the skill necessary to do this exercise correctly. It is well worth it. Women, who have always had problems with the lower tummy bulge, will love this. In the advanced workout, this exercise becomes Jackknives, an military favorite. A healthy back is a must for this very intense exercise.

8) Crunches

This is the most simple and effective upper abdominal conditioning exercise. Crunches should only be done as prescribed in this program and are made more effective without using your hands to lift your head. This will condition the abs and all the muscles connected to your head. If you feel strain in your neck, it is probably because your neck muscles are weak and need conditioning. Having written that I will add that you should use discretion and assess your ability on a day-to-day basis. Do not force the issue of doing crunches. Take it one day at a time and the ability to do this effectively will come to you.

9) Hip Rolls

This is a very simple and effective exercise for the oblique (side) abdominal muscles, the hips and the back. The muscles across the top of the back are flexed isometrically as a result of the elbows pressing to the ground and holding the shoulders in place. A compliment to the rotating effects of the torso during boxing, hip rolls exercise the muscles from the opposite insertion points of boxing. This, as with all the exercises in the EMW, leads to more complete results and a greater balance of functional capacity and fitness.

* Thanks to Health for Life.

10) Marching
This style of marching is designed to fatigue the legs, abs, hips and rotating torso muscles (obliques) as well as provide an aerobic effect on the body. This type of aerobic fatigue process will make the specific leg, abdominal, hip and waist exercises more productive when they are done towards the end of the EMW.

11) Calf Raises
I would recommend doing the EMW barefoot on a carpeted surface. This will give the muscles of the feet an opportunity to be exercised without the encumbrance of shoes. Many weightlifters train barefoot. Martial Arts have been done for thousands of years barefoot and of course there's gymnastics as well. Flat feet and collapsed arches are commonplace in today's society. I am convinced that this is the result of excessive shoe wear. The inner head of the calf muscles (gastrocnemius and soleus) whose function it is, amongst other things, to stabilize the ankle are underdeveloped in most people. This may be genetics and or a result of shoe wear. Performing calf raises in the prescribed manner will develop the muscles necessary to stabilize your ankle and offset the effects of your shoe wearing habit. I would also encourage you to go barefoot as often as possible to strengthen your feet.

12) Walking
The two segments of walking in the EMW have been strategically placed to allow a respite before the more strenuous segments. Although walking is fantastic exercise, it should not and more importantly, does not constitute and entire exercise program. As I said before, one movement or exercise cannot address all five aspects of total fitness. Still, I would encourage you to walk as much as possible during the course of your day.

Breakdown of the elements

The following graph shows how the EMW is derived from it's elements. The format includes other factors such as following the basic theory of how a workout is done. These factors are Stretch – warm-up – aerobic training – resistance training – cool down – stretch.

The EMW clearly addresses all the elements of a complete fitness program in a simple and effective way. With the added benefits of the Mind/Body Connection and Decompression Mobilization Therapy (DMT), the basic fundamental functional capacity of the body is greatly magnified.

The EMW does not advocate the concept of 'isolation' training. This is a dynamic workout. Isolation exercises, such as are performed by commercially available products, should be used to put the finishing touches to an almost complete physique. Any exercise program or device that advocates and emphasizes the isolation theory as the primary concept has 'put the cart before the horse'. Isolation training which aims to eliminate the muscles surrounding the targeted muscle, has a very low intensity factor and does very little to enhance functional capacity.

The EMW produces maximum intensity by using large groups of muscles. At the same time this enhances the functional capacity of the body. Added to that is the *aerobic into anaerobic exhaustion factor.* This thoroughly fatigues the muscles endurance and then exhausts the muscles with dynamic strength movements. The level of intensity generated as a result of this underscores the philosophy of the program. The EMW is much more effective than any isolation program or device at producing results, functional capacity, fitness and health.

38 ○ Eleven Minute Workout

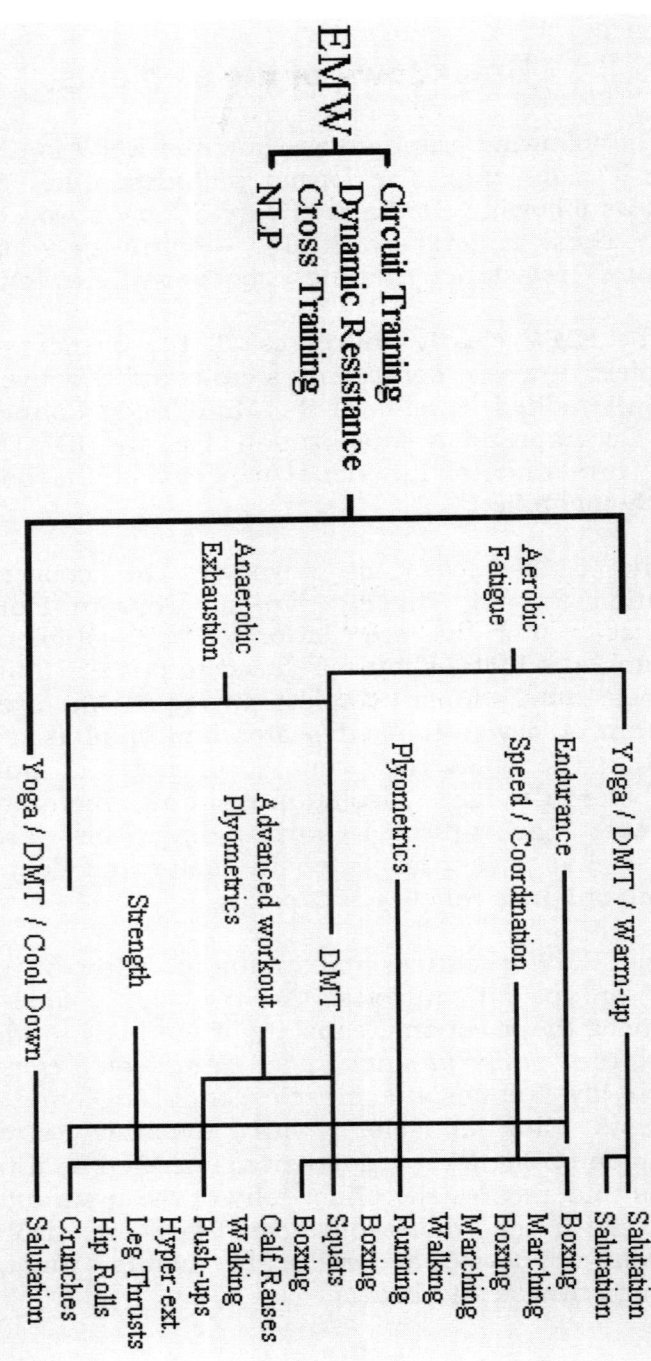

EMW
Beginner Workout

Instructions

For people starting this exercise program, it is recommended that you do this workout for at least four weeks before advancing to the next level

Consult with your doctor before starting this workout program

Salutation

Duration – One minute
The moving into and assuming of each position should take no more than five seconds.

1) Starting position: Standing, feet shoulder width apart, hands together in front of your chest

2) Place your hands in the small of your back with your fingers pointed backwards. Bend your torso and head backwards as far as you can. Keep your knees straight as you do this. Maintain balance.

3) Bend forward at your waist with your knees slightly bent. Let your body, head and arms hang loose.

4) Place your hands on the floor in front of your feet. You may need to bend your knees to do this. Extend your right leg backwards as far as possible with your knee on the floor.

5) As you look down you will see your two hands and one foot. Lift the hand by your foot and reach up as high as you can while you spread your fingers and look up as well.

6) Return your hand to the ground. Turn your head forward as you extend your other leg back. Keep your arms straight as you lower your hips to the floor. Both knees are on the floor.

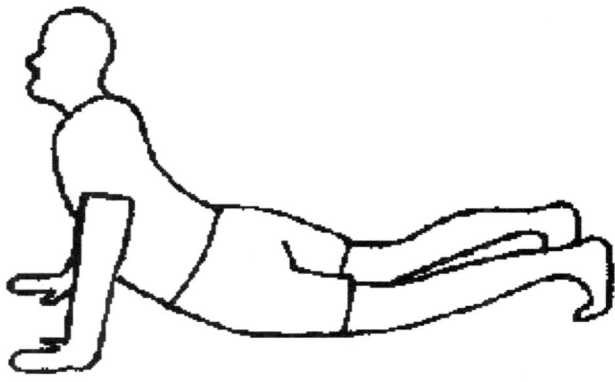

7) Keeping your arms straight, lift your hips up as high as possible as you straighten your legs. Press your head down between your arms as far as you can.

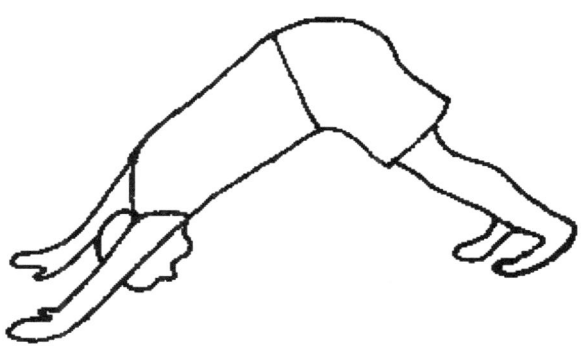

8) Lower your hips and knees to the floor while keeping your arms straight. Lift your head.

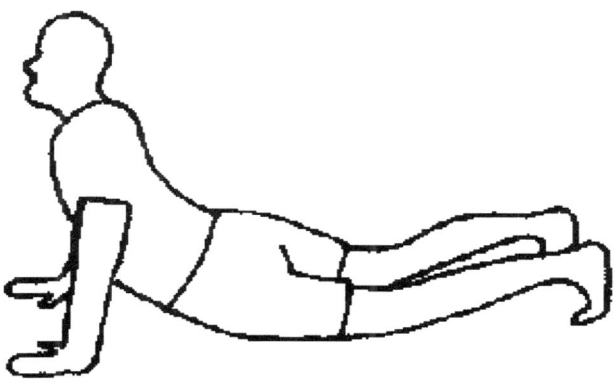

9) Bring your right leg forward and place your foot behind your hand with your back knee on the floor. Once again raise the hand by your foot. Extend it directly upwards, spread your fingers and turn your head up.

10) Turn your head down and replace your hand in front of your foot.

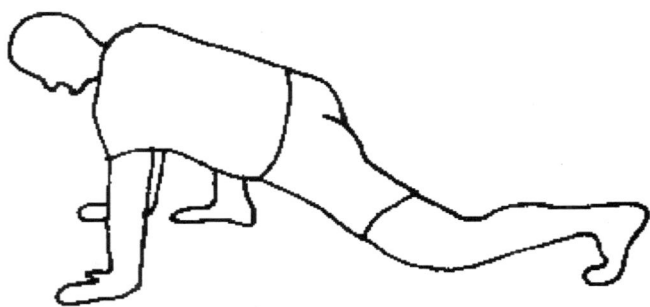

11) Bring your other leg forward and place your foot behind your hand. Straighten your legs until your body, head and arms hang forward. Keep your legs slightly bent.

12) Straighten up slowly and carefully. Place your hands in the small of your back again with your fingers pointed backwards. Bend your head and torso back as far as possible. Keep your knees straight and maintain balance.

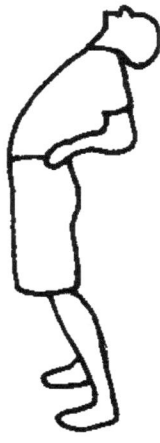

13) Straighten up and bring your hands together in front of you. The Salutation is complete. Move immediately into the next Salutation.

The duration is one minute.
Repeat the movements exactly as described.

Beginner Workout instructions ○ **47**

Salutation
Duration – One minute – Clockwise from the top.

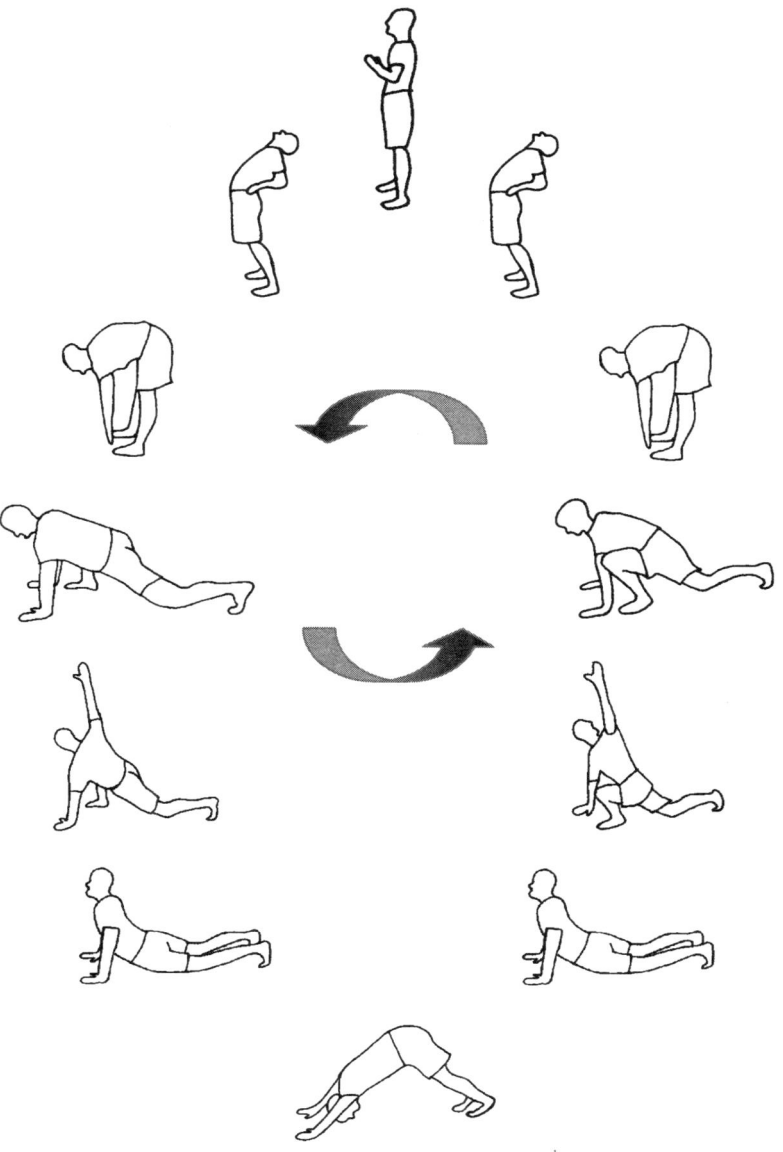

BEGIN NEXT EXERCISE IMMEDIATELY

Boxing

Duration – 30 seconds
Starting Position: Feet wide apart, knees slightly bent. Hold your fists at your chin.

Muscle Focus
- All torso, arm and waist muscles -

1) Keep your feet firmly planted on the ground.
2) Punch straight ahead, alternating the hands in rapid succession.
3) Extend each arm until it is straight and quickly pull it back.
4) Continue for 30 seconds and....

BEGIN NEXT EXERCISE IMMEDIATELY

Beginner Workout instructions ○ **49**

Marching

Duration – 30 seconds
Starting position: Standing, arms at your sides

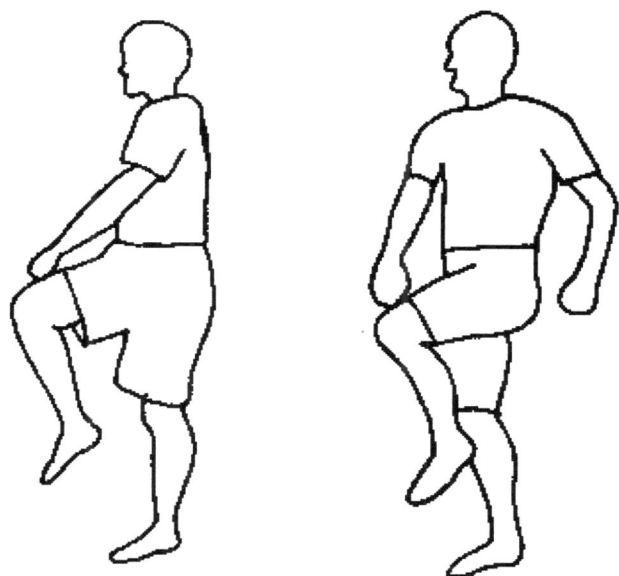

Muscle Focus
- **Legs, hips and lower abdominals** -

1) March in place and touch each hand to the opposite knee in rapid succession.
2) Continue for 30 seconds and...

BEGIN NEXT EXERCISE IMMEDIATELY

Boxing

Duration – 30 seconds
Starting Position: Feet wide apart, knees slightly bent. Hold your fists at your chin.

Muscle Focus
- All torso, arm and waist muscles -

1) Keep your feet firmly planted on the ground.
2) Punch straight ahead, alternating the hands in rapid succession.
3) Extend each arm until it is straight and quickly pull it back.
4) Continue for 30 seconds and....

BEGIN NEXT EXERCISE IMMEDIATELY

Marching

Duration – 30 seconds
Starting position: Standing, arms at your sides

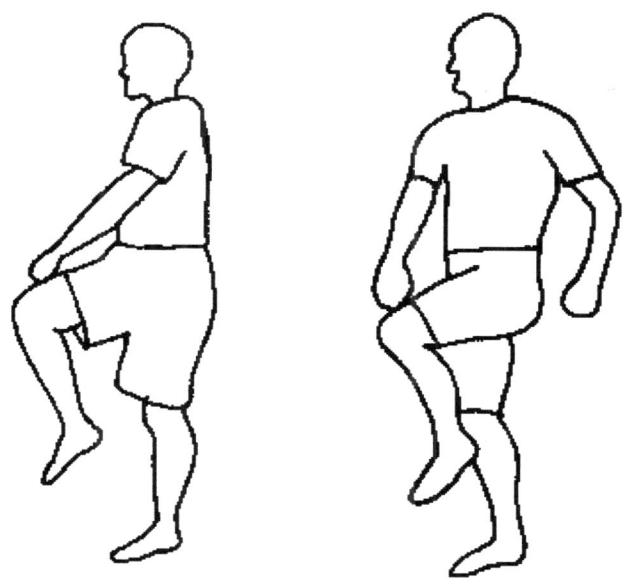

Muscle Focus
- Legs, hips and lower abdominals -

1) March in place and touch each hand to the opposite knee in rapid succession.
2) Continue for 30 seconds and...

BEGIN NEXT EXERCISE IMMEDIATELY

Walking

Duration – 30 seconds
Starting position: Standing with your arms at your sides.

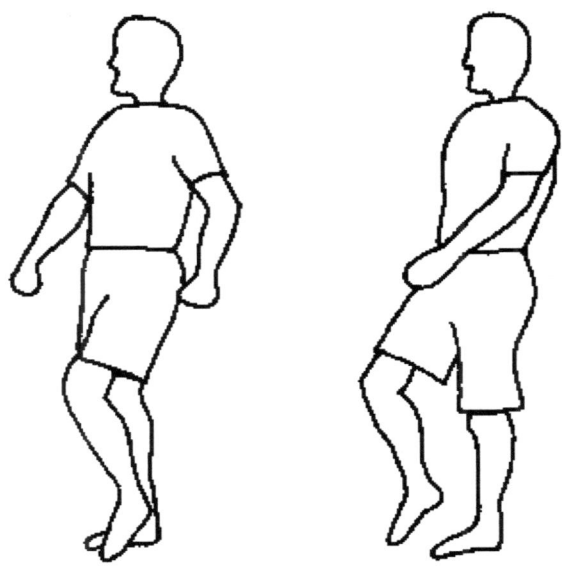

**Muscle Focus
- The whole body -**

1) Walk in place, swing arms, breathe deeply and relax.
2) Continue for 30 seconds and....

BEGIN NEXT EXERCISE IMMEDIATELY

Beginner Workout instructions ○ **53**

Running

Duration – 30 seconds
Starting position: Standing, fists clenched against your chest.

Muscle Focus
- Legs, hips, buttocks and abdominals -

1) Run in place keeping your fists against your chest.
2) Your feet should just clear the floor.
3) Continue for 30 seconds and...

BEGIN NEXT EXERCISE IMMEDIATELY

Boxing

Duration – 30 seconds
Starting Position: Feet wide apart, knees slightly bent. Hold your fists at your chin.

Muscle Focus
- All torso, arm and waist muscles -

1) Keep your feet firmly planted on the ground.
2) Punch straight ahead, alternating the hands in rapid succession.
3) Extend each arm until it is straight and quickly pull it back.
4) Continue for 30 seconds and....

BEGIN NEXT EXERCISE IMMEDIATELY

Squats

Duration: 30 seconds
Starting Position: Standing, feet shoulder width apart, arms at your sides.

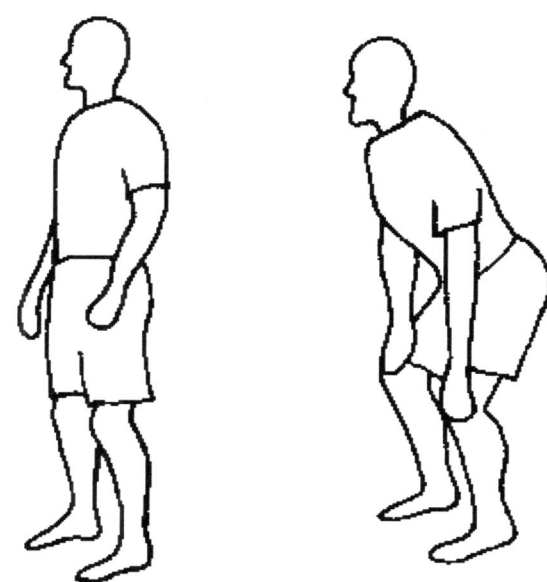

Muscle Focus
- Legs, hips, buttocks and lower back -

1) This movement is exactly like sitting down in a chair and then standing up again.
2) Push your butt out and lean your body forward as you bend your knees.
3) This is necessary to keep your heels on the floor at all times.
4) Place your hands on your knees as you lower yourself.
5) At this point push off with your hands and stand up.
6) Continue for 30 seconds and...

BEGIN NEXT EXERCISE IMMEDIATELY

Boxing

Duration – 30 seconds
Starting Position: Feet wide apart, knees slightly bent. Hold your fists at your chin.

Muscle Focus
- All torso, arm and waist muscles -

1) Keep your feet firmly planted on the ground.
2) Punch straight ahead, alternating the hands in rapid succession.
3) Extend each arm until it is straight and quickly pull it back.
4) Continue for 30 seconds and....

BEGIN NEXT EXERCISE IMMEDIATELY

Calf Raise

Duration – 30 seconds
Starting Position: Standing, feet apart, arms at your sides.

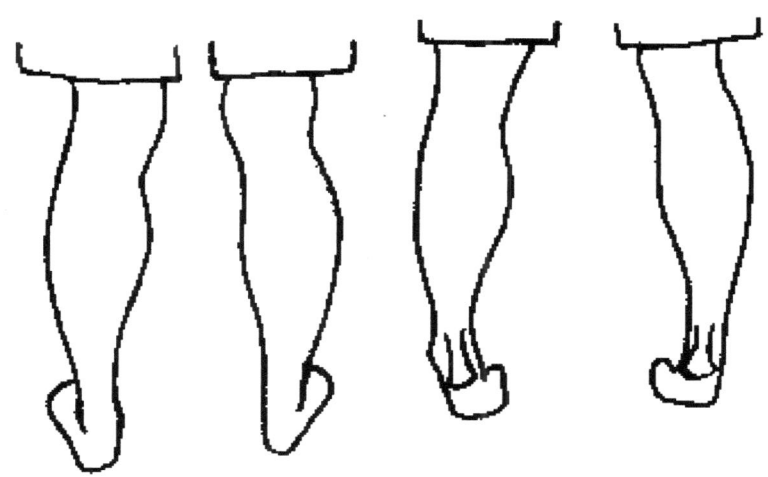

Muscle Focus
- The calf muscles -

1) Raise up on your toes as high as possible and then lower to the starting position.
2) Repeat in a slow controlled manner.
3) Your weight should be felt on the outer edges of your feet.
4) This is accomplished by rolling your ankles out as you raise up.
5) Continue for 30 seconds and....

BEGIN NEXT EXERCISE IMMEDIATELY

Walking

Duration – 30 seconds
Starting Position: Standing with your arms at your sides.

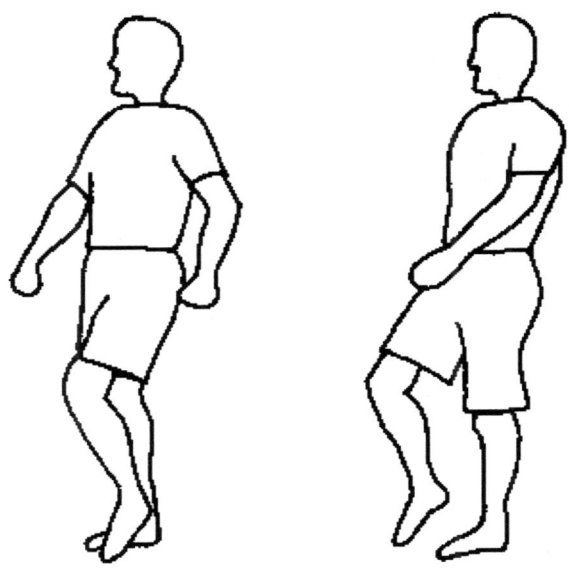

Muscle Focus
- The whole body -

1) Walk in place, swing arms, breathe deeply and relax.
2) Continue for 30 seconds and....

BEGIN NEXT EXERCISE IMMEDIATELY

Push-ups

Duration – 30 seconds
Starting Position: Your knees and hands are on the floor with your arms straight. Keep your body straight from knees to shoulder.

**Muscle Focus
- Chest, shoulders and Triceps -**

1) Bend your arms and lower your body towards the floor.
2) Push your body up by straightening your arms.
3) When starting out, you do not have to lower yourself all the way to the floor. Short movements will build strength and in time you will be able to get all the way to the floor.
4) Continue for 30 seconds and....

BEGIN NEXT EXERCISE IMMEDIATELY

Hyper Extensions

Duration – 30 seconds
Starting Position: Lying on your stomach. Place your hands on your buns. Your legs are straight and together.

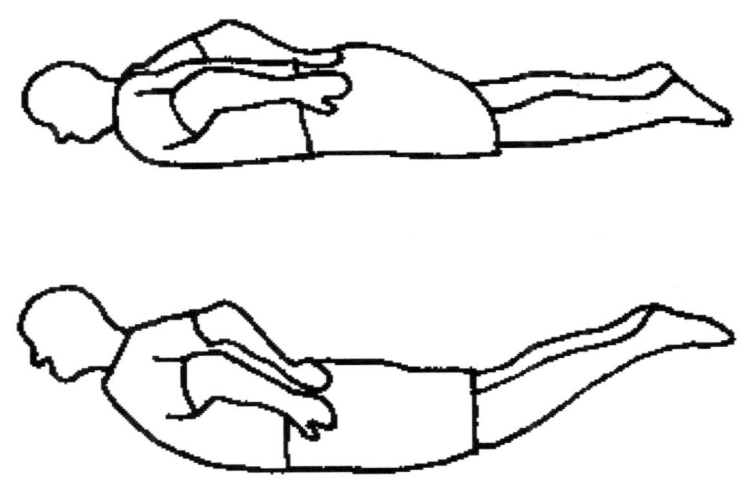

Muscle Focus
- Neck, back, buttocks, hamstrings -

1) In a smooth controlled manner, lift your head, shoulders and legs just a few inches off the floor.
2) Squeeze your buttocks to lift your legs. Keep your legs straight and together as you do this.
3) Lower to the floor and repeat.
4) Continue for 30 seconds and...

BEGIN NEXT EXERCISE IMMEDIATELY

HFL Leg Thrusts

Duration – 30 seconds
Starting Position: Lying on the floor with your legs raised. Tuck your fists under your tailbone to keep your lower back in contact with the floor.

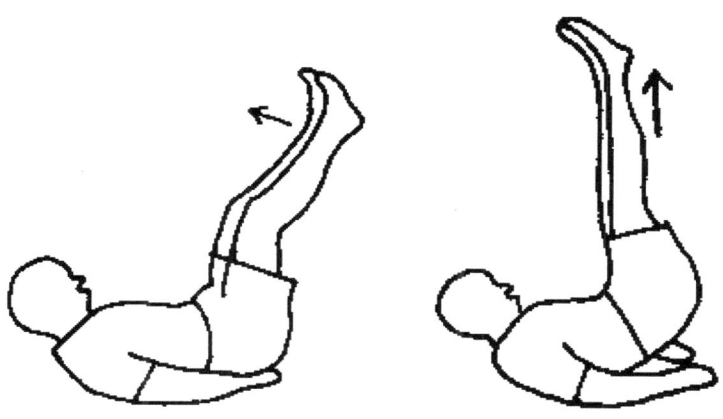

Muscle Focus
- Abdominals -

1) If possible, lift your head and shoulders until your chin is on your chest. This requires abdominal strength and will make the exercise harder.
2) Your legs should be near vertical with your lower back in contact with the floor.
3) In one smooth movement lift your legs until vertical and then thrust your legs and hips up and off your hands.
4) Lower your hips and then your legs to the original position and repeat.
5) Continue for 30 seconds and...

BEGIN NEXT EXERCISE IMMEDIATELY

Hip Rolls

Duration – 30 seconds
Starting Position: Lie on your back, bend your knees and keep your feet on the floor. Press your elbows onto the floor to keep your shoulders on the floor.

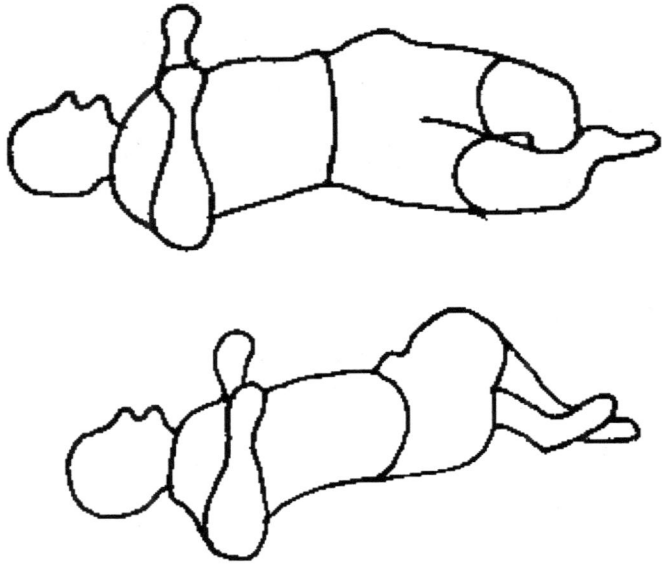

Muscle Focus
- Obliques, hips, lower and upper back -

1) Lower your knees to one side and to the floor if possible.
2) Lift the knees up and over to the floor on the opposite side and continue back and forth.
3) Keep your feet on the floor at all times.
4) Continue for 30 seconds and...

BEGIN NEXT EXERCISE IMMEDIATELY

Beginner Workout instructions ○ **63**

Crunches

Duration – 30 seconds
Starting Position: Lie on your back with your knees bent and your feet flat on the floor.

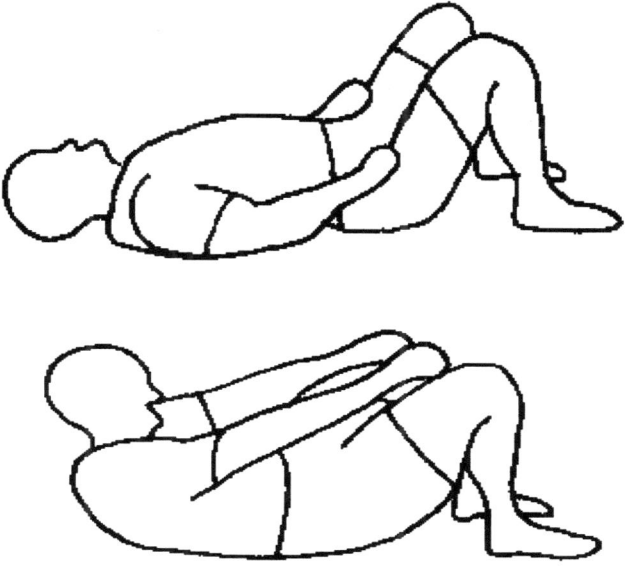

Muscle Focus
- Abdominals -

1) Lift your head and shoulders as you reach up to touch your hands on your knees.
2) Lower to the floor and repeat.
3) Continue for 30 seconds and...

BEGIN NEXT EXERCISE IMMEDIATELY

Salutation

Duration – One minute – Clockwise from the top.

That concludes the Beginner workout.

An important reminder

If you are just starting an exercise program, stay on the Beginner workout for at least four weeks before trying the Intermediate workout. This will give your body a chance to become conditioned to the new routine. Once you start the Intermediate workout, be aware of the 'hump' that generally occurs during the next four weeks. It's the point at which most people quit. Be mindful of negative thoughts that will start creeping into your head. The urge to skip workouts and procrastinate. Excuses about how you feel. A sense of complacency. Thinking that you deserve a day off because you are doing so well. Your schedule might get hectic and your first thoughts will be about putting off the workout until tomorrow. You might have to go out of town for a few days. Anything and everything will suddenly become a major obstacle.

Now that I have brought this to your attention, you are ready and mentally prepared to overcome this 'hump'. Overcoming this 'hump' will clear the path for you to establish exercise as part of your daily routine. Remember the path I wrote about on the inside cover? It will get better so stay on the path.

EMW Intermediate Workout

Instructions

Recommended for those that have completed at least four weeks of the Beginner workout are physically active or play sports

Consult with your doctor before starting this workout program

Salutation

Duration – One minute – Clockwise from the top.

Repeat Salutation—Begin next exercise immediately.

Boxing

Duration – 30 seconds
Starting Position: Feet wide apart, knees slightly bent. Hold your fists at your chin.

Muscle Focus
- All torso, arm and waist muscles -

1) Keep your feet firmly planted.
2) Punch straight ahead, alternating the hands in rapid succession.
3) Extend each arm until it is straight and pull the elbow all the way back behind the shoulder before the next punch is thrown. This will cause your body to twist at the waist.
4) Continue for 30 seconds and....

BEGIN NEXT EXERCISE IMMEDIATELY

Intermediate Workout instructions ○ **69**

Marching

Duration – 30 seconds
Starting position: Standing, arms at your sides

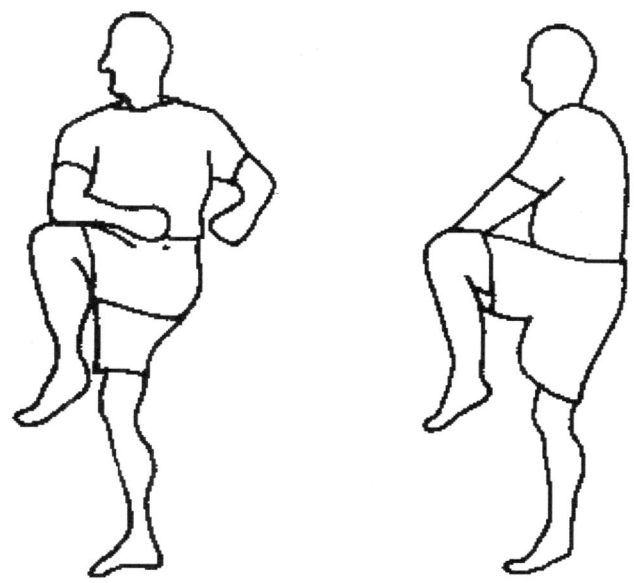

Muscle Focus
- Legs, hips and lower abdominals -

1) March in place and touch each elbow to the opposite knee in rapid succession.
2) Continue for 30 seconds and...

BEGIN NEXT EXERCISE IMMEDIATELY

Boxing

Duration – 30 seconds
Starting Position: Feet wide apart, knees slightly bent. Hold your fists at your chin.

Muscle Focus
- **All torso, arm and waist muscles** -

1) Keep your feet firmly planted.
2) Punch straight ahead, alternating the hands in rapid succession.
3) Extend each arm until it is straight and pull the elbow all the way back behind the shoulder before the next punch is thrown. This will cause your body to twist at the waist.
4) Continue for 30 seconds and....

BEGIN NEXT EXERCISE IMMEDIATELY

Marching

Duration – 30 seconds
Starting position: Standing, arms at your sides

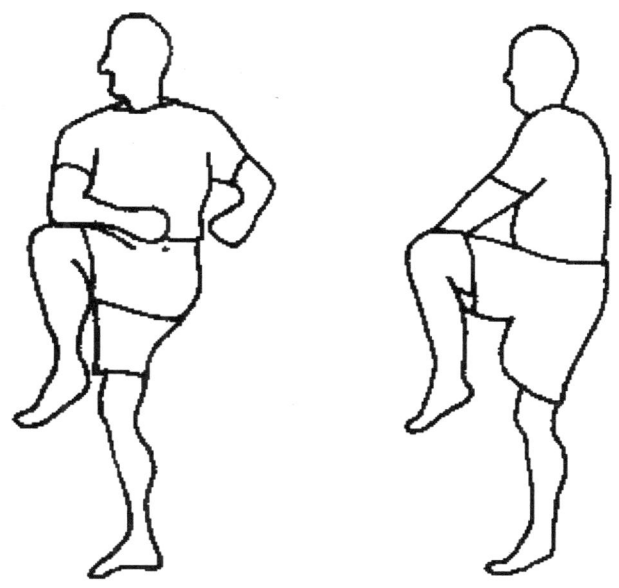

Muscle Focus
- Legs, hips and lower abdominals -

1) March in place and touch each elbow to the opposite knee in rapid succession.
2) Continue for 30 seconds and...

BEGIN NEXT EXERCISE IMMEDIATELY

72 ○ Eleven Minute Workout

Walking

Duration – 30 seconds
Starting Position: standing with your arms at your sides.

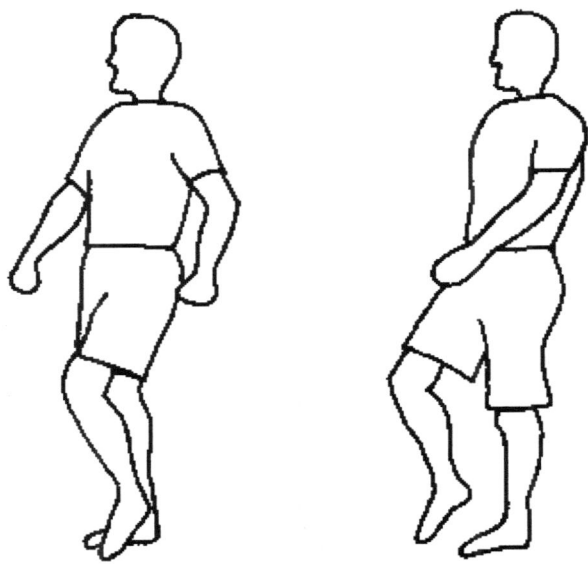

Muscle Focus
- The whole body -

1) Walk in place, swing arms, breathe deeply and relax.
2) Lift your knees until your thighs are at least 45 degrees to the floor.
3) Continue for 30 seconds and....

BEGIN NEXT EXERCISE IMMEDIATELY

Intermediate Workout instructions ○ **73**

Running

Duration – 30 seconds
Starting position: Standing, fists clenched against your chest.

**Muscle Focus
- Legs, hips, buttocks and abdominals -**

1) Run in place keeping your fists against your chest.
2) Lift your knees forward until your thighs are at least 45 degrees to the floor.
3) Continue for 30 seconds and...

BEGIN NEXT EXERCISE IMMEDIATELY

Boxing

Duration – 30 seconds
Starting Position: Feet wide apart, knees slightly bent. Hold your fists at your chin.

Muscle Focus
- All torso, arm and waist muscles -

1) Keep your feet firmly planted
2) Punch straight ahead, alternating the hands in rapid succession.
3) Extend each arm until it is straight and pull the elbow all the way back behind the shoulder before the next punch is thrown. This will cause your body to twist at the waist.
4) Continue for 30 seconds and....

BEGIN NEXT EXERCISE IMMEDIATELY

Intermediate Workout instructions ○ **75**

Squats

Duration: 30 seconds
Starting Position: Standing, feet shoulder width apart, arms at your sides.

Muscle Focus
- Legs, hips, buttocks and lower back -

1) This movement is exactly like sitting down in a chair and then standing up again.
2) Push your butt out and lean your body forward as you bend your knees.
3) This is necessary to keep your heels on the floor at all times.
4) Place your hands on your knees as you lower yourself until your thighs are parallel to the floor.
5) At this point push off with your hands and stand up.
6) Continue for 30 seconds and...

BEGIN NEXT EXERCISE IMMEDIATELY

Boxing

Duration – 30 seconds
Starting Position: Feet wide apart, knees slightly bent. Hold your fists at your chin.

Muscle Focus
- All torso, arm and waist muscles -

1) Keep your feet firmly planted
2) Punch straight ahead, alternating the hands in rapid succession.
3) Extend each arm until it is straight and pull the elbow all the way back behind the shoulder before the next punch is thrown. This will cause your body to twist at the waist.
4) Continue for 30 seconds and....

BEGIN NEXT EXERCISE IMMEDIATELY

Calf Raise

Duration – 30 seconds
Starting Position: Standing, feet apart, arms at your sides.

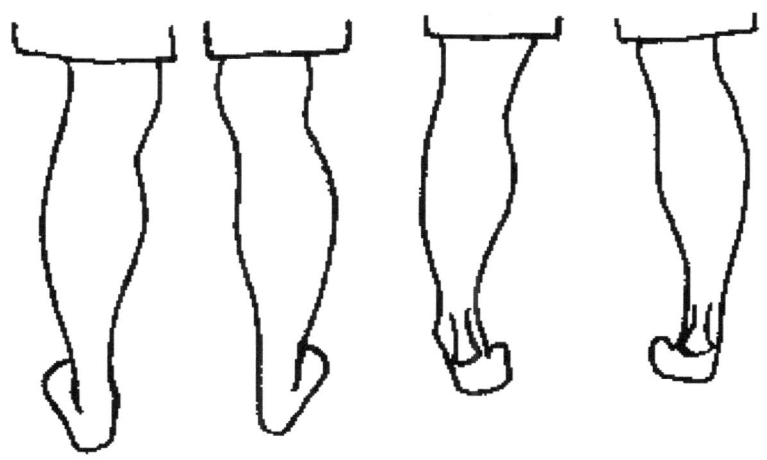

Muscle Focus
- The calf muscles -

1) Raise up on your toes as high as possible and then lower in a controlled manner.
2) Repeat in rapid succession.
3) Your weight should be felt on the outer edges of your feet.
4) This is accomplished by rolling your ankles out as you raise up.
5) Continue for 30 seconds and....

BEGIN NEXT EXERCISE IMMEDIATELY

Walking

Duration – 30 seconds
Starting Position: standing with your arms at your sides.

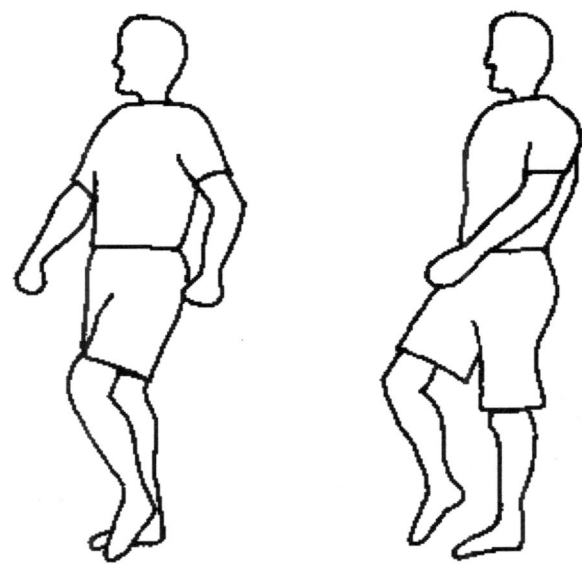

Muscle Focus
- The whole body -

1) Walk in place, swing arms, breathe deeply and relax.
2) Lift your knees until your thighs are at least 45 degrees to the floor.
3) Continue for 30 seconds and....

BEGIN NEXT EXERCISE IMMEDIATELY

Push-ups

Duration – 30 seconds
Starting Position: Your feet and hands are on the floor with your arms and legs straight. Keep your body straight from your feet to your shoulders.

Muscle Focus
- Chest, shoulders and Triceps -

1) Bend your arms and lower your body towards the floor.
2) Push your body up by straightening your arms.
3) When starting out, you do not have to lower yourself all the way to the floor. Short movements will build strength and in time you will be able to get all the way to the floor.
4) Continue for 30 seconds and....

BEGIN NEXT EXERCISE IMMEDIATELY

Hyper Extensions

Duration – 30 seconds
Starting Position: Lying on your stomach. Your arms are extended directly sideways. Your legs are straight and together.

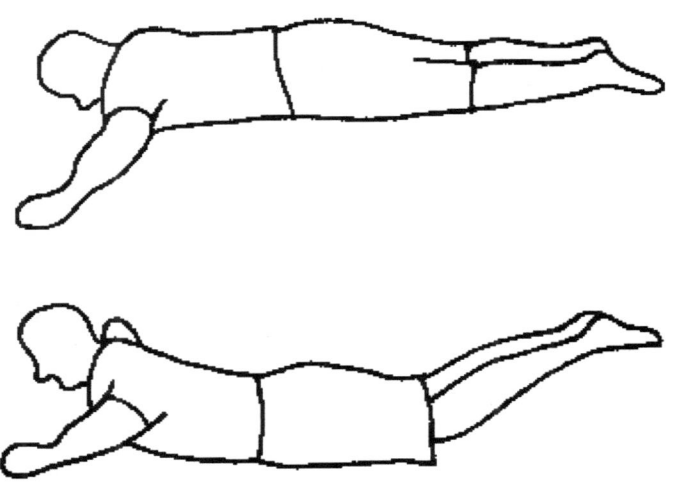

Muscle Focus
- Neck, back, buttocks, hamstrings -

1) In a smooth controlled manner, lift your head, shoulders and legs just a few inches off the floor.
2) Squeeze your buttocks to lift your legs. Keep your legs straight and together as you do this.
3) Lower to the floor and repeat.
4) Continue for 30 seconds and...

BEGIN NEXT EXERCISE IMMEDIATELY

HFL Leg Thrusts

Duration – 30 seconds
Starting Position: Lying on the floor with your legs raised. Tuck your fists under your tailbone to keep your lower back in contact with the floor.

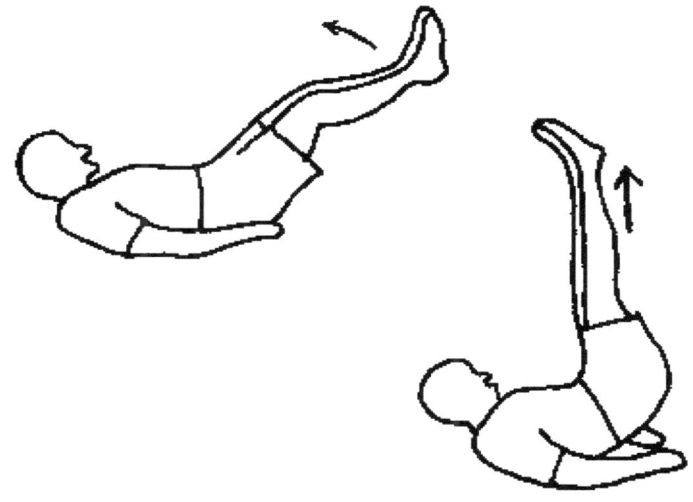

Muscle Focus
- Abdominals -

1) Lift your head and shoulders until your chin is on your chest. This requires abdominal strength and will make the exercise harder.
2) Your legs should be at 45 degrees with your lower back in contact with the floor.
3) In one smooth movement lift your legs until vertical and then thrust your legs and hips up and off your hands.
4) Lower your hips and then your legs to the original position and repeat.
5) Continue for 30 seconds and...

BEGIN NEXT EXERCISE IMMEDIATELY

Hip Rolls

Duration – 30 seconds
Starting Position: Lie on your back, bend your knees and keep your feet on the floor. Press your elbows onto the floor to keep your shoulders on the floor.

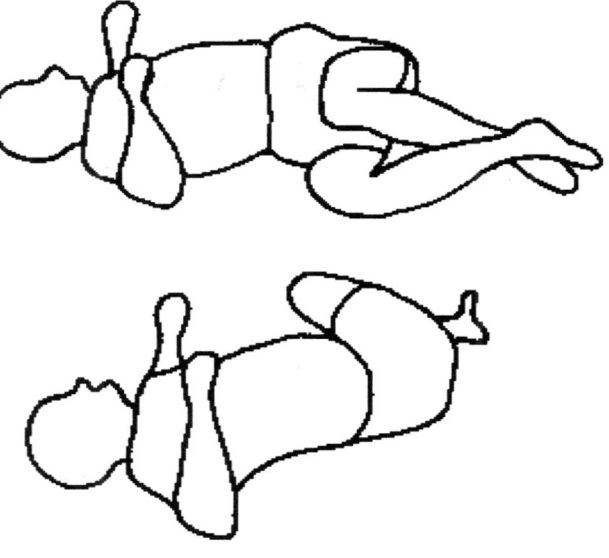

Muscle Focus
- Obliques, hips, lower and upper back -

1) Lower your knees to one side and to the floor if possible.
2) Lift the knees up and over to the floor on the opposite side and continue back and forth.
3) Keep your feet off the floor at all times.
4) Continue for 30 seconds and...

BEGIN NEXT EXERCISE IMMEDIATELY

Crunches

Duration – 30 seconds
Starting Position: Lie on your back with your knees bent and your feet flat on the floor.

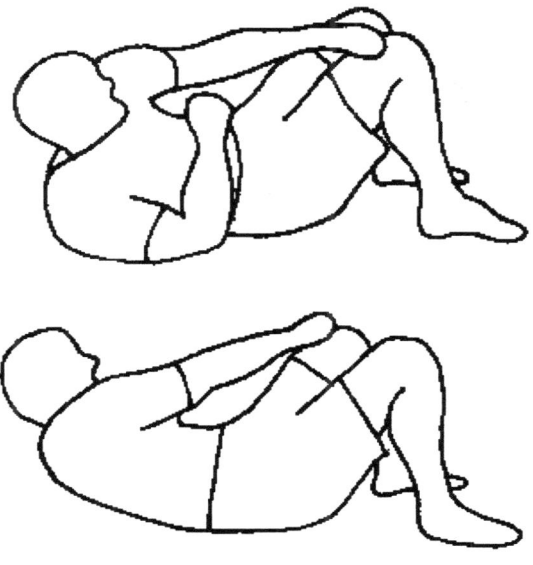

Muscle Focus
- Abdominals -

1) Lift your head and shoulders as you reach up to touch your LEFT hand to your right knee.
2) Lower to the floor and repeat movement by touching your RIGHT hand to your left knee.
3) Continue touching your hands to the opposite knees in rapid succession for 30 seconds and…

BEGIN NEXT EXERCISE IMMEDIATELY

Salutation

Duration – One minute – Clockwise from the top.

This concludes the Intermediate workout.

EMW
Advanced Workout

Instructions

Recommended for those that have completed at least four weeks of the two previous levels or for the serious athlete

Consult with your doctor before starting this workout program

Salutation

Duration – One minute – Clockwise from the top.

Repeat Salutation—Begin next exercise immediately.

Advanced Workout instructions ○ **87**

Boxing

Duration – 30 seconds
Starting Position: Feet wide apart, knees slightly bent. The right fist is at your chin and the other is behind your back.

Muscle Focus
- All torso, arm and waist muscles -

1) Keep your feet firmly planted.
2) Punch straight ahead using only the RIGHT hand.
3) Extend the arm until it is straight and pull the elbow all the way back behind the shoulder before the next punch is thrown. This will cause your body to twist at the waist.
4) Continue for 30 seconds and....

BEGIN NEXT EXERCISE IMMEDIATELY

Marching

Duration – 30 seconds
Starting position: Standing, arms at your sides

Muscle Focus
- Legs, hips and abdominals -

1) Lift one leg straight forward and touch your toe with the opposite hand.
2) Lower your leg to the floor and repeat movement with your opposite leg and arm.
3) A slight bend in both legs is acceptable.
4) Continue alternating for 30 seconds and...

BEGIN NEXT EXERCISE IMMEDIATELY

Advanced Workout instructions ○ **89**

Boxing

Duration – 30 seconds

Starting Position: Feet wide apart, knees slightly bent. The left fist is at your chin and the other is behind your back.

Muscle Focus
- All torso, arm and waist muscles -

1) Keep your feet firmly planted.
2) Punch straight ahead using only the LEFT hand.
3) Extend the arm until it is straight and pull the elbow all the way back behind the shoulder before the next punch is thrown. This will cause your body to twist at the waist.
4) Continue for 30 seconds and....

BEGIN NEXT EXERCISE IMMEDIATELY

Marching

Duration – 30 seconds
Starting position: Standing, arms at your sides

Muscle Focus
- Legs, hips and abdominals -

1) Lift one leg straight forward and touch your toe with the opposite hand.
2) Lower your leg to the floor and repeat movement with your opposite leg and arm.
3) A slight bend in both legs is acceptable.
4) Continue alternating for 30 seconds and...

BEGIN NEXT EXERCISE IMMEDIATELY

Advanced Workout instructions ○ 91

Walking

Duration – 30 seconds
Starting Position: standing with your arms at your sides.

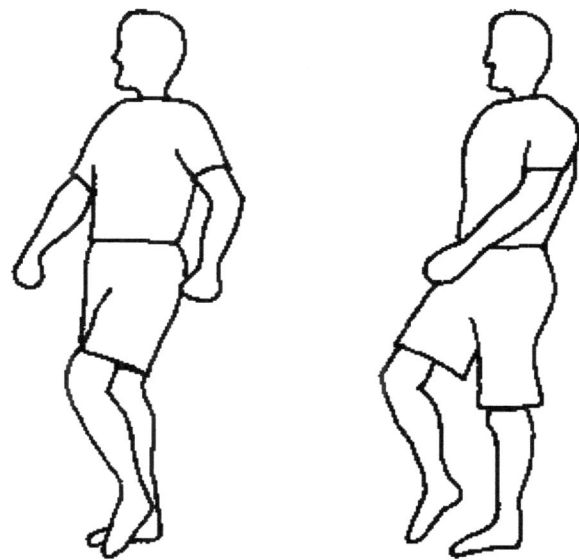

Muscle Focus
- The whole body -

1) Walk in place, swing arms, breathe deeply and relax.
2) Lift your knees until your thighs are parallel to the floor.
3) Continue for 30 seconds and....

BEGIN NEXT EXERCISE IMMEDIATELY

Running

Duration – 30 seconds
Starting position: Standing, fists clenched against your chest.

Muscle Focus
- Legs, hips, buttocks and abdominals -

1) Run in place keeping your fists against your chest.
2) Lift your knees forward until your thighs are parallel to the floor.
3) Continue for 30 seconds and...

BEGIN NEXT EXERCISE IMMEDIATELY

Advanced Workout instructions ○ **93**

Boxing

Duration – 30 seconds
Starting Position: Feet wide apart, knees slightly bent. The right fist is at your chin and the other is behind your back.

Muscle Focus
- All torso, arm and waist muscles -

1) Keep your feet firmly planted.
2) Punch straight ahead using only the RIGHT hand.
3) Extend the arm until it is straight and pull the elbow all the way back behind the shoulder before the next punch is thrown. This will cause your body to twist at the waist.
4) Continue for 30 seconds and....

BEGIN NEXT EXERCISE IMMEDIATELY

Squats

Duration: 30 seconds
Starting Position: Standing, feet shoulder width apart, arms at your sides.

Muscle Focus
- Legs, hips, buttocks and lower back -

1) Lower yourself until your thighs are parallel to the floor and then jump as high as you can.
2) Upon landing, immediately lower yourself until your thighs are parallel to the floor again and repeat movement.
3) Use your hands on your knees to push off.
4) Continue for 30 seconds and...

BEGIN NEXT EXERCISE IMMEDIATELY

Advanced Workout instructions ○ **95**

Boxing

Duration – 30 seconds
Starting Position: Feet wide apart, knees slightly bent. The left fist is at your chin and the other is behind your back.

Muscle Focus
- All torso, arm and waist muscles -

1) Keep your feet firmly planted.
2) Punch straight ahead using only the LEFT hand.
3) Extend the arm until it is straight and pull the elbow all the way back behind the shoulder before the next punch is thrown. This will cause your body to twist at the waist.
4) Continue for 30 seconds and....

BEGIN NEXT EXERCISE IMMEDIATELY

Calf Raise

Duration – 30 seconds
Starting Position: Standing, feet apart, arms at your sides.

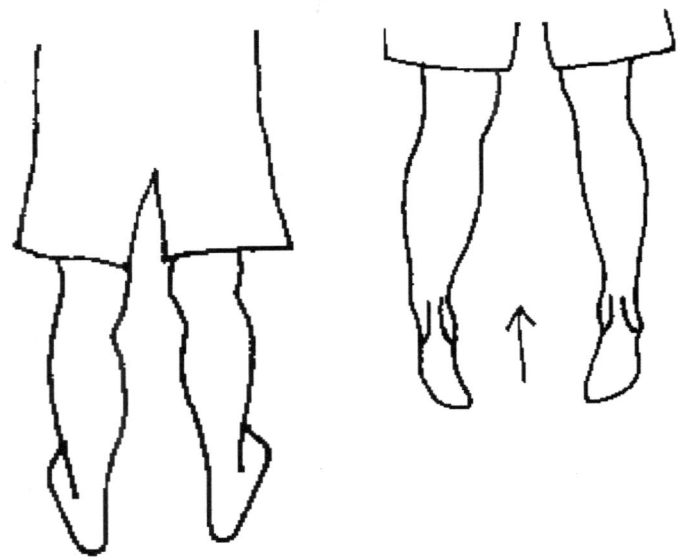

Muscle Focus
- Calf muscles -

1) Bounce up and down on your toes.
2) Your feet should clear the floor on each bounce.
3) Use knee flexion to absorb the impact upon landing.
4) Continue for 30 seconds and...

BEGIN NEXT EXERCISE IMMEDIATELY

Walking

Duration – 30 seconds
Starting Position: standing with your arms at your sides.

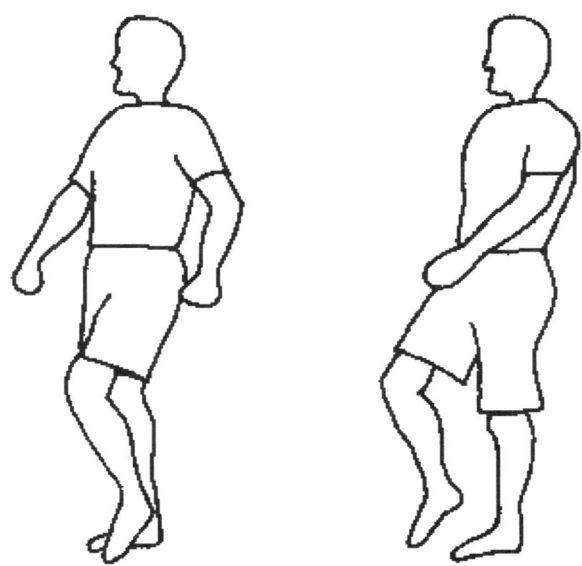

Muscle Focus
- The whole body -

1) Walk in place, swing arms, breathe deeply and relax.
2) Lift your knees until your thighs are parallel to the floor.
3) Continue for 30 seconds and....

BEGIN NEXT EXERCISE IMMEDIATELY

Push-ups

Duration – 30 seconds

Starting Position: Your feet and hands are on the floor with your arms bent. Keep your body straight from your feet to your shoulders.

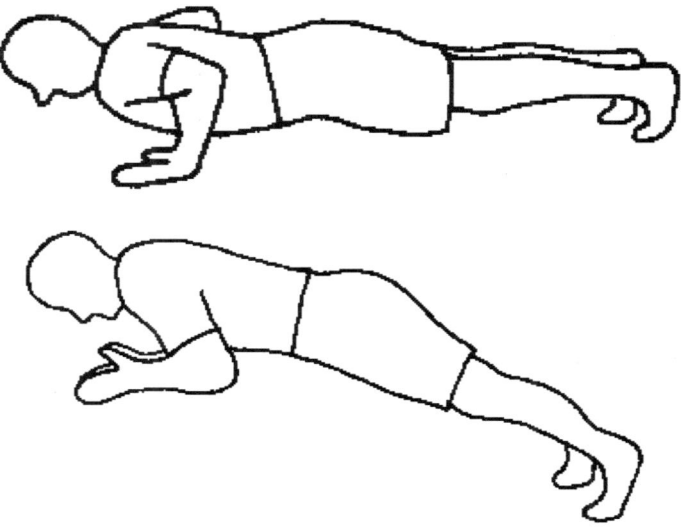

Muscle Focus
- Chest, Shoulders, triceps and abdominals -

1) Push up hard enough to clear the floor and clap your hands together before returning to the starting position.
2) Stop your body from flopping to the floor on the way down.
3) Lower in a controlled manner and then repeat in rapid succession.
4) Continue for 30 seconds and...

BEGIN NEXT EXERCISE IMMEDIATELY

Advanced Workout instructions ○ **99**

Hyper Extensions

Duration – 30 seconds
Starting Position: Lying on your stomach. Your arms are extended directly forward. Your legs are straight and together.

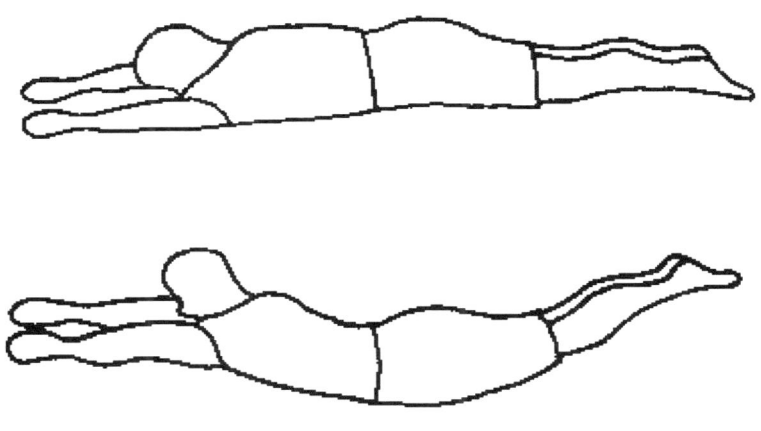

Muscle Focus
- Neck, back, buttocks, hamstrings -

1) In a smooth controlled manner, lift your head, shoulders and legs just a few inches off the floor.
2) Squeeze your buttocks to lift your legs. Keep your legs straight and together as you do this.
3) Lower to the floor and repeat.
4) Continue for 30 seconds and...

BEGIN NEXT EXERCISE IMMEDIATELY

Jackknives

Duration – 30 seconds
Starting Position: Lying on your back. Legs and arms are straight and together.

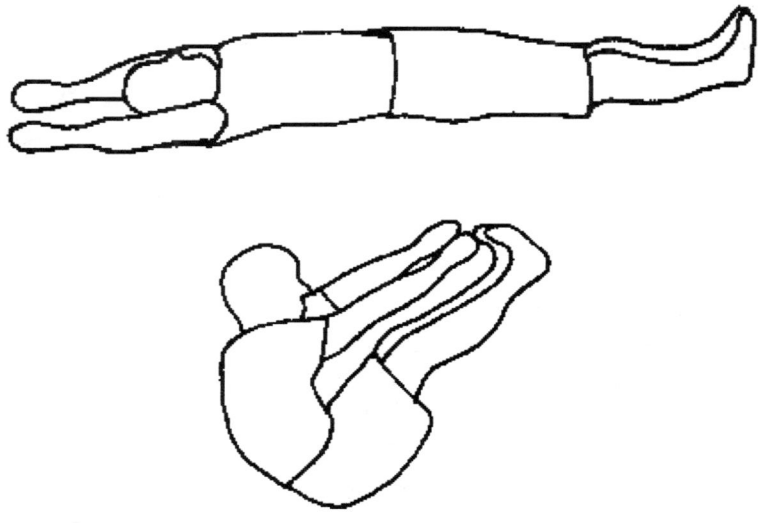

Muscle Focus
- Abdominals -

1) Sit up and at the same time lift both legs and touch the toes in a pike position.
2) Lower to the floor in a smooth controlled manner.
3) Your arms should be kept straight and a slight bend in the knees is acceptable.
4) Your back and legs should clear the floor on each repetition.
5) Continue for 30 seconds and...

BEGIN NEXT EXERCISE IMMEDIATELY

Hip Rolls

Duration – 30 seconds
Starting Position: Lie on your back, keep your legs straight and crossed at your ankles. Press your elbows onto the floor to keep your shoulders on the floor.

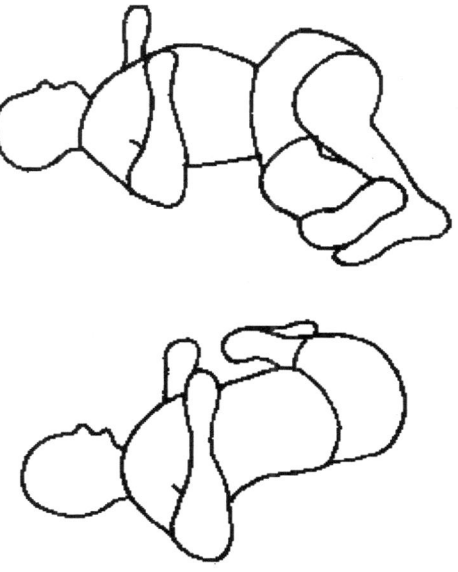

Muscle Focus
- Obliques, hips, lower and upper back -

1) Lift your legs until vertical and then lower to one side and touch the floor.
2) Immediately lift your legs up and over to touch the floor on the other side.
3) Keep your elbows and shoulders pressed to the floor.
4) Continue back and forth for 30 seconds and...

BEGIN NEXT EXERCISE IMMEDIATELY

Crunches

Duration – 30 seconds
Starting Position: Lie on your back with your knees bent and your feet flat on the floor.

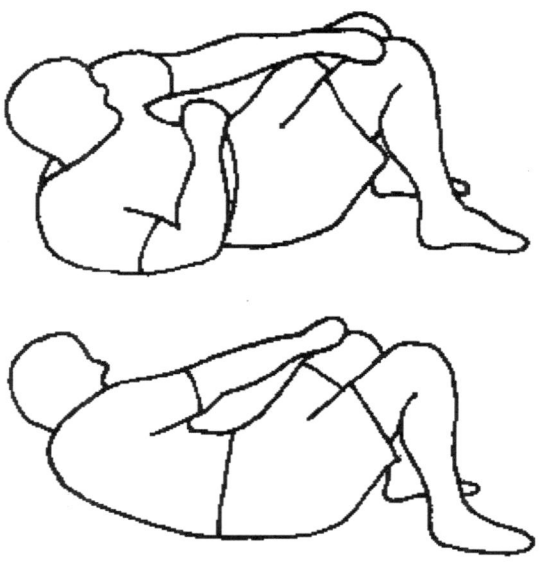

Muscle Focus
- Abdominals -

1) Lift your head and shoulders as you reach up to touch your LEFT hand to your right knee.
2) Do not lower to the floor. Repeat movement by touching your RIGHT hand to your left knee.
3) Continue touching your hands to the opposite knees in rapid succession for 30 seconds and...

BEGIN NEXT EXERCISE IMMEDIATELY

Advanced Workout instructions ○ **103**

Salutation
Duration – One minute – Clockwise from the top.

This concludes the advanced workout.

The recipe for success

Getting the most out of an exercise program is dependant on certain factors that greatly enhance the possibility of success. The following points I am going to share with you can be applied to this program or any other.

Firstly, there are very few of us that have the desire to get up for working out every day. Cover yourself by having a few workout partners. Our natural competitive urge is stimulated and on those days that you don't feel like exercising, you can have your workout partners motivate you. Secondly, do your workout first thing in the morning. Then it's done and you don't have to think about it until tomorrow. Thirdly, above all else, exercise technique is paramount. The risk of injury is greatly reduced and the probability of getting results is greatly increased. Below is a simple formula to follow.

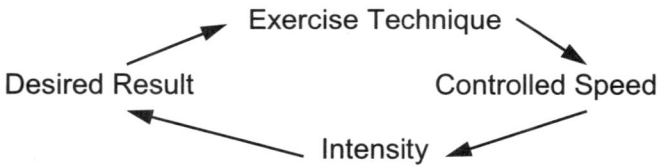

Lastly, remember that the results are not attained in one workout. Exercise moderately hard every day. Having to take a day off to recover is a sure sign that you overdid it the day before.

The three levels of the EMW quite clearly define which category you are in. It would be prudent to complete at least four weeks at any level before progressing to the next. Do not rush to the next level. In fact, once you have moved up, you can always do the previous level or two on any given day. Remember that the most important factor is daily exercise.

The Mind/Body Connection in fitness

Some years ago I met Cardell Smith. His passion and belief Neuro Linguistic Programming and it's application to life are absolutely awe inspiring. After many hours of intense conversation, I had grasped the concept and was ready to apply is valuable knowledge to my life.

It was during this time that I owned the Strauss Fitness Center in Los Angeles. I had opened this private training facility for my clients and helped them get results from their training in the quickest way possible. Still, I was always on the lookout for ways and methods to improve. Things fell right into place when I started to add NLP to my personal training. I called Cardell and asked his opinion on the matter. He said that if the correct principles of NLP were applied, it should work!'

I carefully selected and chose to approach only a handful of the clients I had worked with. With confidentiality assured I unveiled my plan. The results were instantaneous and dramatic. I am now going to reveal this secret which has remained until the writing of this book.

Exercise has always been promoted as a mindless concept. Watching TV, having a conversation or hearing some trainer scream 'one more rep' is the way most everyone is doing it. Counting repetitions is commonplace. Besides the obvious stimuli from doing the repetitions, how does counting enhance the workout. Well it doesn't, not one little bit. It all hot air and a waste of valuable oxygen.

The process of counting does not effectively utilize the power of the mind during the exercise performance. It is true that the body can only do what the mind commands and it's ability to function without the mind is zero.

Here is where NLP comes in. By replacing these useless numbers with distinct commands or specifically what I call three word 'mantras', the body receives the stimuli through the neuron pathways to implement the result of the command. As you hear the commands you give your body, they are delivered through the ear canal to the Hypothalamus gland, located just beneath the brain and are then converted into chemicals. These chemicals are delivered to their destination by the nervous system. The endings of the nervous system are in the muscles. This is where we want the mantras to end up. Each time the mantra is voiced, the neuron pathway, which is established between the brain and the muscles, is reinforced and strengthened.

Here then are some mantras that you can be used.
During the Salutation:
    Perfect Flexibility Now, Healthy Body Now,
    Strong Body Now, or any combination of these.
During the exercises:
    1st Word: Perfect, Healthy, Strong
    2nd Word: Arms, Back, Chest, Abs etc.
    3rd Word: Now!

During the salutation, voice one command per position. In the boxing, marching, walking and running segments, voice the words on the cadence of one limb only, otherwise you might hyperventilate. In the course of the other exercises, voice the words on the lifting part of the movement. Once you get to the advanced version, every other rep might be appropriate.

Since the body cannot decide for itself and is at the mercy of the brain, it will accept and implement the commands without question. The result will be whatever your concept of a perfect, strong and healthy body is. The verbal commands add a unique dimension of psychosomatics to the EMW.

Tracking your progress

The following charts represent three months. I suggest that you mark the day and month you start working out. Every day you do the workout, put a check mark on the calendar. This will track your consistency. When you see the boxes filling up with check marks, you will feel a sense of accomplishment and pride in your efforts. Remember that the most important factor is to workout every day. Tracking your workouts in this way will help you develop the all important habit of working our every day.

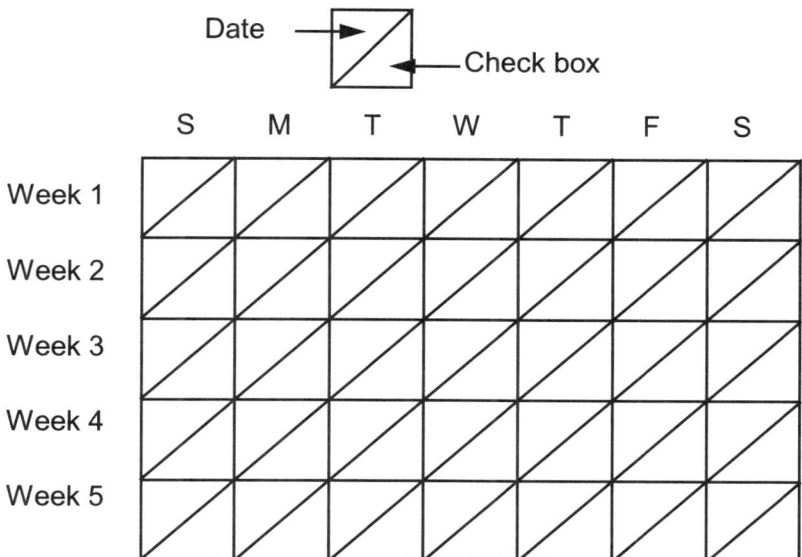

First Month: Total Workouts =
Divide by 4 for weekly average =

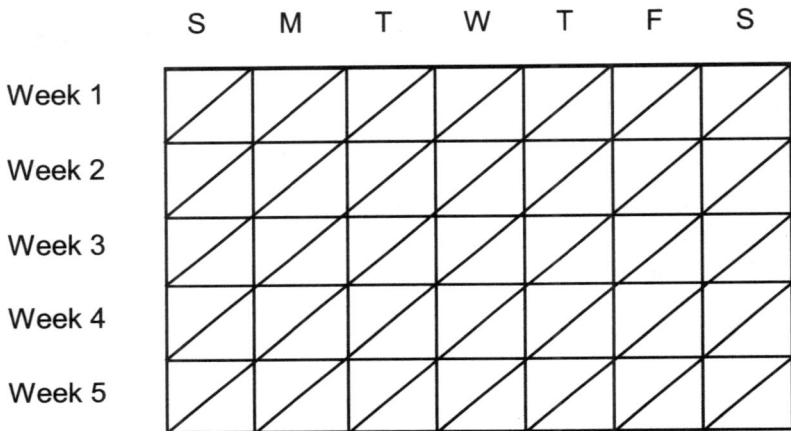

Second Month: Total Workouts =
Divide by 4 for weekly average =

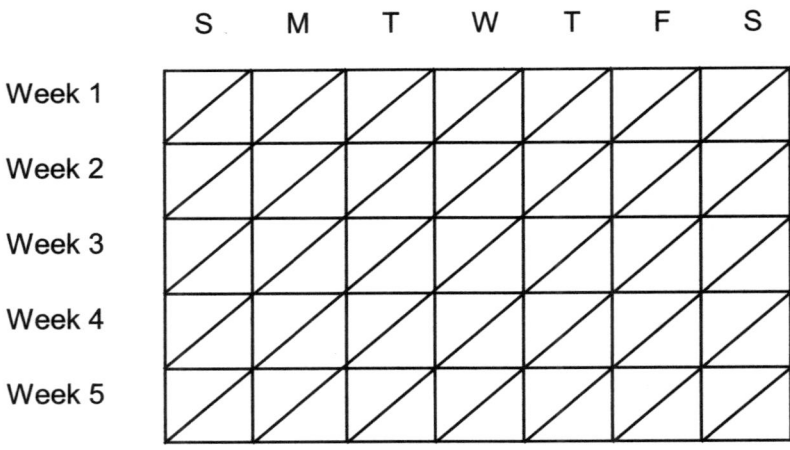

Third Month: Total Workouts =
Divide by 4 for weekly average =

The purpose of the three month charts is once again to help you get over the 'hump' that usually occurs somewhere between week four and eight. Persevering through this point is critical to either making or breaking the habit of exercise. Trust me, you'll be all smiles on the other side. It's not to say that you wont have results before that but as I said before, the best results come with a long term commitment and developing exercise as part of your daily routine.

The EMW progress potential

So just what kind of progress can your expect from the EMW? The following chart demonstrates the progress potential when all the elements of the EMW are implemented.

This progress is defined in the total number of repetitions completed during the EMW, which will determine the Intensity level. The results are toned and firm muscles that are metabolically active and burn calories 24 hours a day.

Once again it is advisable to use discretion in the pursuit of Intensity. Each time you do the workout, do so to the best of your ability and don't compromise anything for the sake of more reps. In time they will come. Just let it happen.

The chart below is designed to give you some idea of the total number of repetitions that can be completed in the EMW.

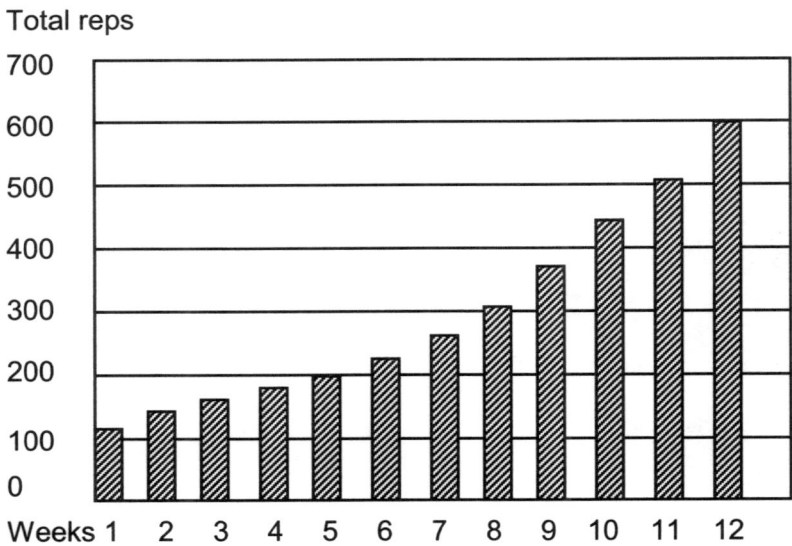

Stress and Exercise

Quite simply, stress is energy and more importantly it is good energy. Let me explain. First: stress is the result of external 'force' which then becomes an internal energy as the result of certain physiological manifestations. The demands placed on us in our day-to-day activities produces stress. This is defined as '... a state in which a strong demand is made on the nervous system'. Hence the term 'nervous breakdown' which is when the accumulation of stress overtakes the nervous system and the body breaks down.

Second: let's define the nervous system. It is '...the system in humans comprising of the brain, the spinal cord, the ganglia (a center of industrial force or activity), the motor and sensory nerves and their endings that serve to produce **muscular activity** on the basis of stimuli received and interpreted by the brain'.

Take a moment to digest that and even re-read the first two paragraphs. Stress results in the nerve endings (called synapses) firing in the muscles and trying to produce muscular contractions. Hello! Muscular contractions? Sounds just like what we need for a good workout.

At this point you have certain choices. You can reach for an alcoholic drink, a cigarette or gorge yourself with food and ultimately do more damage to yourself. The other choice is to channel the stress into a comprehensive exercise program such as the EMW and use stress to your advantage. I think you will be pleasantly surprised at the results.

We can't avoid stress but we can decide what to do with it.

Diet and Exercise

I think that it's fair to say that the results of any exercise program including the EMW, can be enhanced by a diet that coincides with your goal and the exercise program. This I proved to myself during my years as a competitive bodybuilder. So just what sort of diet is best for the EMW? So many books have been written on the subject and more are sure to come. Each one of them has value.

In order for your body to change the way you want it to depends on three factors that are equally important and inseparable. They are exercise, diet and rest. Unless these are combined, the results in any one of them is limited. Yes, what I'm saying is that the EMW should be combined with diet and adequate rest.

Diet will feed the body with the nutrients it needs to replenish itself from exercise, stress and daily living. This all takes place while you sleep. So once again I say that the three factors are combined and no one is more important than the other. My gift to you is the EMW. The other two you must take care of yourself. Get plenty of sleep and control what goes into your mouth.

Empower yourself with knowledge about your body. The best book I have read is "The Human Fuel Handbook, Nutrition for Peak Athletic Performance" from Health for Life. In a simple and clear manner it will explain what happens from the moment you put food in your mouth until it comes out on the other end. After reading this book you will have a clear understanding of how your body utilizes food and what to expect from what you eat.

Do your research if you decide to take any supplements to make sure it is right for you.

Using vitamin and mineral supplements wisely*

Vitamins and minerals are substances your body needs in small amounts for normal growth, function and health. Together, vitamins and minerals are called micronutrients. Your body can't make most micronutrients, so you must get them from the foods you eat or, in some cases, from supplements.

You need vitamins for normal body functions, mental alertness and resistance to infection. They enable your body to process proteins, carbohydrates and fats.

Your body also needs minerals. The Major minerals are important in the development and health of your bones and teeth; regulating the water and chemical balance in your body; for normal growth and health.

Supplements are not substitutes. They can't replace the hundreds of nutrients in whole foods you need for a nutritionally balanced diet Whole foods — fruits, vegetables, grains, lean meats and dairy products — have three main benefits you can't find in a pill: Whole foods are complex, provide dietary fiber, contain other substances that may be important for good health.

Guidelines for good nutrition*

Every day your body requires a certain amount of energy from carbohydrates, protein and fats to function properly. Because no single food provides all of the nutrients your body needs, eating a variety of foods ensures that you get all of the necessary nutrients and other substances associated with good health.

In general follow national dietary recommendations as a guide when planning your daily meals and snacks. If you need to lose or gain weight, some of these recommendations may need to be adjusted and you should consult a registered dietitian or your doctor.

*Mayo Clinic guidelines

Additional Tips

The most important tip I can give you is to get yourself as many workout partners as possible. Whether it is family members or friends your natural competitive urge is stimulated and you can draw off their energy. This is especially helpful on days that you don't feel like exercising. Arnold himself was known to have a different training partner for each body part and they would rotate through the gym all day long. Each one providing him with a fresh challenge for his workouts. This I believe was instrumental in his success as a bodybuilder.

I suggest doing the EMW first thing in the morning. It will leave you feeling refreshed and with more energy after the workout than before you started. Doing it after work will melt away stress and tension from your body allowing you to relax and enjoy a good night's rest.

I suggest doing the EMW barefooted on a carpeted surface. For reasons that I stated before, the muscles in your feet will get the exercise they need.

A great way to increase the Intensity of your workout is to add resistance, such as a weighted glove. By adding 1-2 Lbs. per hand, you increase the amount of weight moved with each repetition.

References

American Medical News, August 16, 1993, v36 n31 p5 (1) Charles Culhane

Health Facts, Sept 1993 v18 n172 pl (2)

Health for Life, Secrets of Advanced Bodybuilders, 1985 Health for Life

Legendary Abs II, Health for Life 1989, Health for Life

Decompression Mobilization Therapy, Robert M. Martin II, DMT – TM

Treat Your Own Back, Robin McKenzie, 1996

Tufts University Diet and Nutrition Letter, Oct 1993 v11 n8 pl (1)

Royal Canadian Air Force, Exercise Plans for Physical Fitness, Pocket Books, A division of Simon & Schuster Inc. N.Y., N.Y.

Mayo Clinic. www.mayoclinic.com

Suggested Reading

The Human Fuel Handbook, Nutrition for Peak Athletic Performance, written by Health for Life, Los Angeles, 1988

Synershape, A Scientific Weight Loss Guide, written by Health for Life, Los Angeles 1984

Oxygen Therapies, Ed McCabe, Energy Publications, Morrisville, NY 1988

Treat Your Own Back, Robin McKenzie, 1985 Spinal Publications, New Zealand.

DMT: Decompression Mobilization Therapy, Robert M. Martin II, Pasadena, California.

Sports Supplement Review, 3rd Issue, by Bill Phillips, Mile High Publishing, Golden, Colorado.

Juicing For Life, Cherie Calborn and Maureen Keene, Avery Publishing Group.

Glossary

Abdominals: The muscles of the stomach.

Aerobics: System of exercise based on increasing oxygen intake to stimulate heart and lung activity.

Anaerobic: System of exercise requiring less oxygen uptake and relying more on muscle strength, e.g. Powerlifting.

Calisthenics: The exercise of the body and limbs to promote strength, coordination, speed and endurance.

Circuit Training: Timed sequence of a variety of exercises.

Cross Training: Combining exercise forms for maximum and complete fitness stimuli.

Decompression Mobilization Therapy: A systematic approach to restoring the function of the Neuro-musculoskeletal system.

Deltoids: The shoulder muscles.

DRM (Dynamic Resistance Movements): Multi-joint movements that utilize the large muscle groups, e.g. Squats.

Endorphins: Naturally occurring morphine like substance secreted by the pituitary gland, to control pain and pleasure.

EMW: Abbreviation for The Eleven Minute Workout.

Erector Spinae: Muscles of the lower back.

Exponentially: Increasing in all directions (in volume).

Fitness: Speed, Coordination, Flexibility, Strength and Endurance.

Functional Capacity: The ability of the body to perform the way it was designed.

Gastrocnemius: The calf muscle, located in the lower part of the leg at the rear.

Glossary

Hamstrings: Muscles located at the rear part of the thigh.

Intensity: How hard the muscles work, at any given point in time in the five categories that make up total fitness.

Isotonic: Constant resistance.

Jab: a short straight punch. The arm is extended straight forward from the body and quickly returned.

Mantra: Positive verbal affirmation and motivation.

Neuron: A nerve cell

Neuro Linguistic Programming: Reprogramming the neuron pathways to establish and/or delete information highways in the body, e.g. habits.

Obliques: The sides of the body, known as the 'love handles'.

Pectorals: The chest muscles.

Plyometrics: Training that uses the myotatic reflex of the muscles to develop explosive eccentric muscle contractions and strength, which is the basis of real athletic power.

Powerlifting: A sport of pure strength. An athlete attempts lifting maximum poundage in one rep. The three exercises are Bench Press, Deadlift and Squats.

Quadriceps: The thigh muscles.

Rhomboids: Muscles located between the shoulder blades. Their function contributes to good posture.

Soleus: A broad flat muscle located beneath the calf muscle.

Synergy: a combination of elements created to produce a whole greater than the sum of the elements.

Vertebrae and Disks: Bones of the spine.

VRI: Volume of Repetition Intensity.

Online Support

Visit us anytime at our web site for the latest information on health and fitness.

www.11minuteworkout.com

You can also contact Greg for any questions, comments, or additional information on the exercises and a program suited for you.

Email: greg@11minuteworkout.com

Additional Products

The following products are designed to enhance your health and fitness. These items have been selected by Motion Fitness — using a Team of Leading Experts in the Health field to find the best products for you.

Weighted Gloves $19.95

Enhance your workout with these weighted gloves. All of the exercises in the Eleven Minute Workout can be performed using weighted gloves. The additional weight will give you added resistance during movements. Each glove weighs 2LB, and is made of a comfortable Jersey fabric. Great for boxing.

WalkFitness Kit $24.95

Walk <u>10,000 STEPS</u> for your health.
The popular 10,000 step program will help to improve your health. This program was designed by a exercise physiologist and includes: keep fit pedometer, motivational cassette tape, daily log book to record your progress and walk fitness program guide.

Pedometer $19.95

"Keep Fit" pedometer includes easy reading LCD display, a step counter, a mileage display, kilometers, and a calorie counter in sequence making this one of the most complete pedometers on the market. This pedometer also has a unique auto walking and jogging detection sensor. All you have to do is put it on and you're ready to go!

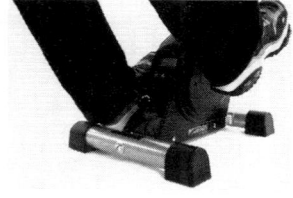

Easy Cycle — $95.00

This mini exercise cycle is ideal for upper and lower body movements. The low impact, adjustable resistance cycle can be used anywhere (chair or table top) for exercise. Now you can get the health benefits of a bicycle, in a compact exercise cycle.

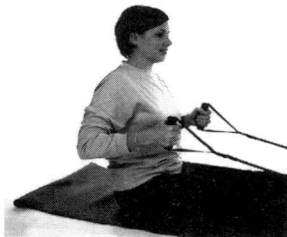

Cord Fitness — From $10.95

Resistance cords are great for toning and strengthening and can be used anywhere. This kit includes: 48" cord with 2 handles, exercise poster, and door anchor.
Light: $10.95, Med.: $11.95, Heavy: $12.95
Kit with all 3 levels: $34.95

Exercise Balls — $24.95

Get a great workout, develop balance and improve flexibility with this Exercise Ball Kit. Includes: burst resistant quality fitness ball, convenient floor pump, and 70 exercise fitness poster.
Specify size: 55cm, 65cm, 75cm

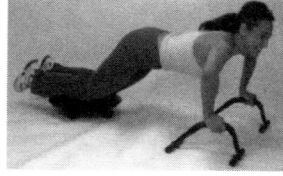

Ultimate Fitness Object — $79.00

By simulating various push-up movements and body extensions, the UFO is a great way to give you that extra edge. It ties in perfectly strength, agility, flexibility into whole body movements. The Ultimate Ab and Torso workout is great for all ability levels. More than 30 innovative exercises.

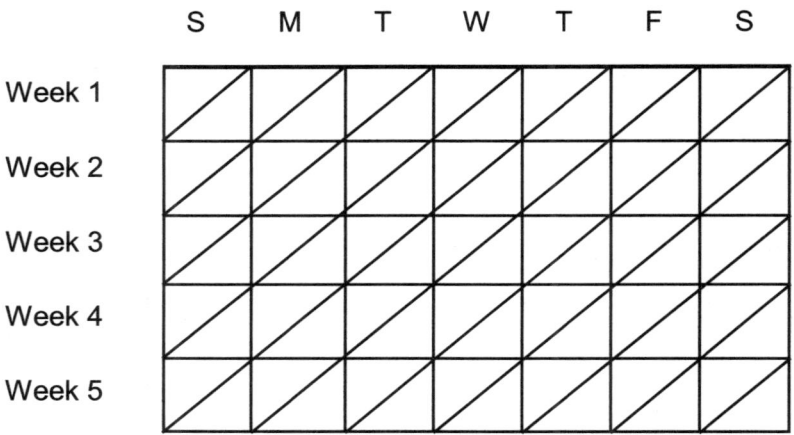

_____ Month: Total Workouts =
Divide by 4 for weekly average =

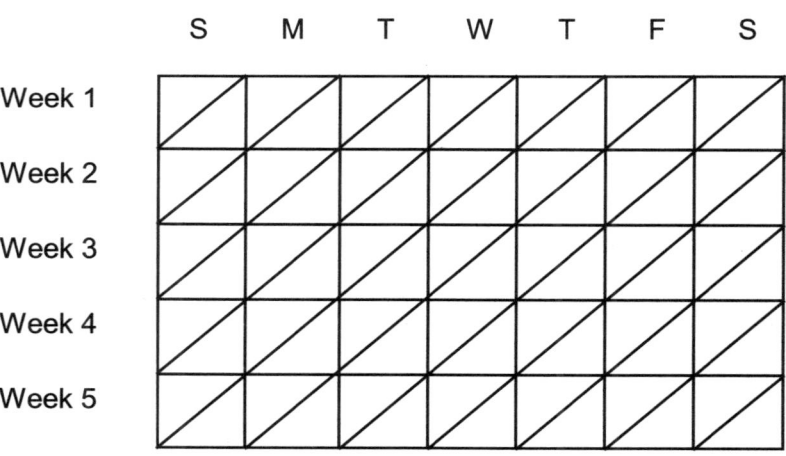

_____ Month: Total Workouts =
Divide by 4 for weekly average =

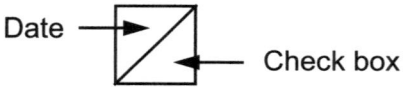

EMW - Progress Chart

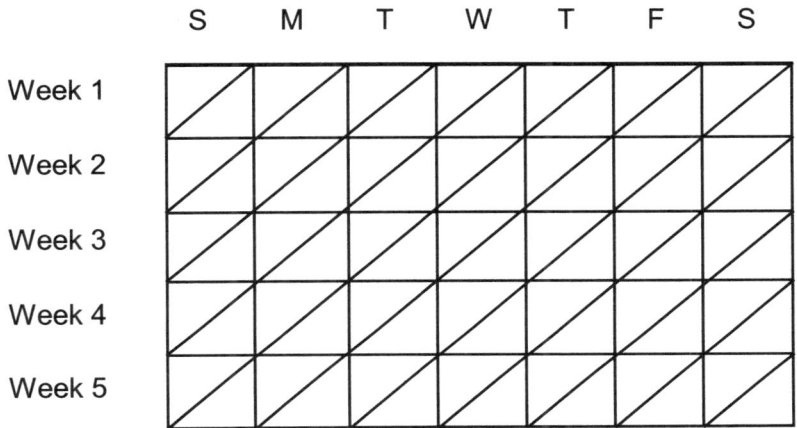

_____ Month: Total Workouts =
Divide by 4 for weekly average =

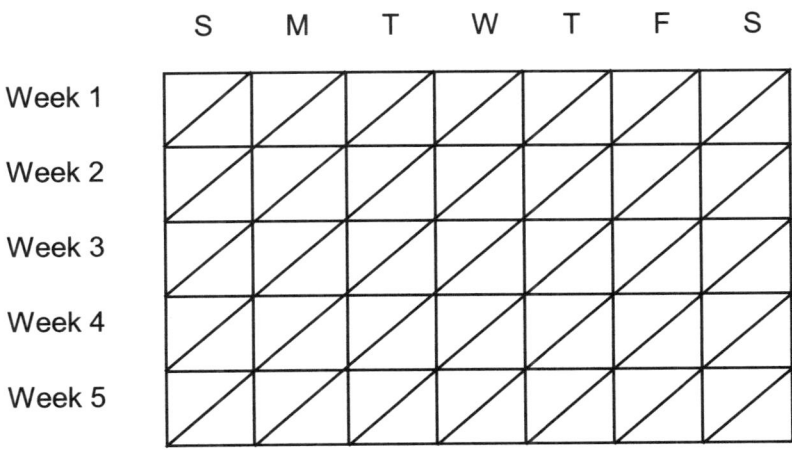

_____ Month: Total Workouts =
Divide by 4 for weekly average =

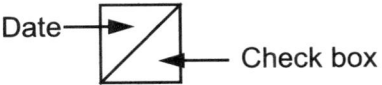

EMW - Progress Chart

**Health & Fitness products
for the whole family**

www.motionfitness.com

Quick Order Form

Fax Orders: 847-963-8966. Send this form.

Telephone Orders: Call 1-877-668-4664 toll free.

Email orders: sales@motionfitness.com

Online orders: www.motionfitness.com

Postal orders: Motion Fitness, 119 E. Palatine Rd #205 Palatine, IL 60067, USA

Please send the following items. I understand that I may return any item for a full refund if not satisfied in 30 days

Item#	Description	Quantity	Cost

Sales tax: Please add 8.75% for items shipped to Illinois.

Shipping: Books-$2.00 for first book, $1.00 for each Addtl.

Shipping: Other items-Free over $100.00 in purchases. $5 charge up to $50 / $10 charge up to $100 in purchases.

Sold to:

Name:	
Address:	
City, State, Zip:	
Telephone:	
Email:	

Payment: Visa   MasterCard   AMEX   Discover

Card Number:			
Name on Card:		Exp. Date:	

Please put me on your mailing list for additional products and educational information:

If you enjoyed this book — Get a copy for a friend!